AF251185

WORKING OUT WHAT GOD WORKS IN

Samuel Chien-Sheng Young

Pacific Press Publishing Association
Mountain View, California
Oshawa, Ontario

DEDICATION

To my parents and my Bible teachers—Pastors Ho Wai Yu, Leung Hing Sun, S.H. Lindt, Giang Chung Kwang, and G.H. Minchin— who each taught me to learn from Christ of God's inward law.

Library of Congress Cataloging in Publication Data

Young, Samuel Chien-Sheng, 1928-
  Working out what God works in.

  Includes bibliographical references.
  1. Christian life—Seventh-Day Adventist authors. 2. Christian ethics—Seventh-Day Adventist authors. I. Title.
BV4501.2.Y67   248.4'8673   81-8658
ISBN 0-8163-0440-8   AACR2

"WORK OUT your salvation with fear and trembling, for it is God who WORKS IN you to will and to act according to his good purpose." Philippians 2:12, 13, NIV, emphasis supplied.

"We must WORK OUT what God WORKS IN"– Testimonies, *vol. 3, p. 381, emphasis supplied.*

"After those days, saith the Lord, I will put my law in their inward parts, and write it in their hearts; and will be their God, and they shall be my people." Jeremiah 31:33.

Contents

The Inward Law

Nearly 2000 years ago, while traveling north to Galilee, the Master rested at a community well on the outskirts of the Samaritan town of Sychar. After His disciples went into town to buy food, a woman of the town came out to the well—a well known widely as being that of the patriarch Jacob. The woman set about doing her routine chore. Seemingly oblivious to His presence, she stepped past the Master to fill her pot with what she thought to be life-giving water.

The Master's constant contact with His Father had sharpened His powers of perception. He saw through the silent reserve of this woman. What He saw was not a haughty Samaritan who spurned the Jews for spurning the Samaritans. Instead He saw a soul devoid of the fruit of the Spirit—shriveled, hungry, dissatisfied. His soul went out to her in love and pity. He longed to offer the genuine water of life, and His mind searched for a common link that could open a channel of communication between them. As she turned to leave, He asked her for a drink—just a drink—and the link was established.

She was startled at the very suggestion that a Samaritan—one of the despised—should serve a Jew! Jews didn't even touch the cups and bowls handled by Samaritans. The questions of Jesus which followed probed deeply, but she feigned to comprehend only the literal meaning and to pass off the obvious intent of the Master's words.

Their brief conversation ranged rapidly through fields of history, genealogy, and the prejudices of race and religion, as the woman moved uneasily under the scrutiny of this remarkable Man. Even so, she was not repelled. He seemed to know even the dark secrets lodged in the deep recesses of her heart and mind. Her concepts of religion and morality were not the same as His. She was in a different world—a world entirely outside that of the Master.

Skillfully, the Master led her into a new relationship with her God. How could she really be very well acquainted with the moral laws God had entrusted to the Jews, so exclusive as to deny contact with the non-Jew as far as possible? Yet in a sense she had, as does each one of us, a set of inward laws—a value system—in the heart.

Christianity is more than a system of rituals—more than mere outward conformity to a set of rules. Christianity is a new relationship between a sinful person and the God who created and sustains him, as the Master showed the Samaritan woman that day so long ago. By His incarnation, Jesus Christ is the direct link between God and man. He is the Substitute and Surety for the sinful race.

In His humanity, by continual dependence upon His heavenly Father, Jesus Christ lived a life utterly devoid of sin. Yet He placed Himself before the law of God as though a sinner, by taking upon Himself the sins of the whole world. He died as the Sin Bearer for all. But the grave could not hold the sinless Sin Bearer; and He came forth a victor over sin, death, the grave, and the devil. His victory made Him our Surety.

Now He offers to sinful men a new-covenant relationship with God by faith in the Substitute and by continual cooperation with the Surety. He takes our sins and gives us His righteousness. We receive this righteousness in two ways. First, in Him we are accounted righteous, and we remain so as long as we maintain our absolute dependence upon Him and His merits. And second, He enters into a living relationship with us whereby the Holy Spirit brings about a new-birth experience in our hearts and minds and writes the law of God—as an inward law—upon the fleshy tables of our hearts. By this inward law all of life is shaped for the believer. He wills to work out what God puts within.

Seldom do we find two people who feel or think alike. In His infinite wisdom, God has created us in such a way that the four and a half billion of us living on earth differ from one another. Yet different as we may be, we are descendants from the same ancestors—Noah and his wife or, even earlier, Adam and Eve.

With all the expanding knowledge cf genetic engineering, it is still a miracle that each baby is born with a unique combination of characteristics and traits unlike those of any other person in the world. Just how God makes this possible remains a mystery to us.

Each child develops a unique sense of good and bad, likes and dislikes—his own inward law—by imitating his closest associates, such as parents, brothers, sisters, and friends. He may in later years model after his heroes, whether an Abraham Lincoln or a Florence Nightingale, an Albert Einstein or a Confucius, a Mahatma Ghandi or a Martin Luther King. And he may accept as his inward law that which is revealed by the God of love and exemplified in the life of Jesus Christ.

Imitation of others, the influences of family religion, education, customs—all may have an impact on the mind of each individual and make his inward law different from those of others. Usually these inward laws retain, as their common elements, some aspects of God's law. But no one completely develops God's law inwardly as a matter of course. Only by coming to Jesus to learn directly of his way of life as revealed by God in the Bible can we come to possess the perfect inward law. God has promised, ''I will put my law in their inward parts, and write it in their hearts; and will be their God, and they shall be my people[1]

Christianity is most concerned with the change in the inner man—a change from the selfish to the godly and godlike. Outward behavior comes from within—one's philosophy, attitudes, and disposition. While the law of the court can regulate only the actions of people, God's law reaches the hidden motives.

Man differs from animals in that his behavior expresses his beliefs and philosophy. Being a free moral agent, man is endowed with the gift of choice and is thus held responsible for his behavior. God will judge man not only because He has given him a conscience—the ability to discern between right and wrong—but also because He has revealed His law through nature, revelation, and the Holy Spirit.

We may redefine sin as ignorance or rejection of God's revelation, and repentance as giving up one's own imperfect inward law and accepting in its place God's perfect law. We may also redefine Christian maturity or sanctification as the process of accepting God's law as ours. Because of the human tendency toward inertia and relapse, the journey to Christian maturity is always slow and rough. It takes a lifetime to internalize some or all of God's law.

Like the Samaritan woman, we are often enslaved by our past experiences and unwilling to change. Only because of God's love and the influence of the Holy Spirit do we ever change. We cannot change by ourselves or write God's law in our own hearts. We can only allow God to write it in our hearts and gratefully allow the Holy Spirit to change our inner motives. Then we may become new creatures—like newborn babes—with gentle hearts that have the ability to learn His perfect law. For God has promised, under the new covenant, "I will put my law in their inward parts, and write it in their hearts; and I will be their God, and they shall be my people."

The Ten Commandment law is the expression of God's character in human terms adapted to our human situation. Hence it is the law of love, for God is love. This law of love is likewise the law of life—the life of God in us.

Basic to human nature and universal in its application is God's law of love. His law transcends all cultures, customs, socioeconomic classes, ages, races, nationalities, times, and geographical locations. It makes Christianity a religion, not of the East or of the West, but of the whole world. So an Asian or an African does not have to accept Western culture when he joins God's family.

Even though we are all different in our cultural heritage, we must still develop the inward law of love according to the high standard taught in the Bible. God can write this law in our hearts only because of the sacrifice Jesus has made for sinners. Although its application may vary with time and location, its essence is universal and unchanging.

From the individual and human viewpoint, there can be no objective values, as is claimed by moral philosophers. At a time when "there was no king in Israel: every man did that which was right in his own eyes."[2] This is still true today. But if the standard of goodness is given by God, who is absolutely objective, then the establishment of a universally objective law is not only possible but sure. Man is the slave of his own experience and temperament, but God's law of love, the "perfect law of liberty"[3] has the power to liberate man from the confines of his ignorance when Christ's sacrifice is accepted as the sinner's basis of acceptance with God.

Though we shall concentrate upon this inward law and its outworking in our individual lives, it is vital that we recognize that the outworking of the inward law does nothing toward earning our salvation.

No matter how perfect our commitment to the inward law and its rule in our lives, we are not equal to the Pattern Man and cannot be. Our obedience, our prayers, our worship, our deeds of love must all be offered up to God with the incense of the righteousness of Christ. They must all be bathed in His precious blood. This alone makes them acceptable with God. This alone brings answers to our prayers.

We will continually need to remind ourselves of these facts, or we will find ourselves slipping into a work-related idea of salvation. We will begin measuring ourselves by ourselves or by one another. Such an effort is not only fruitless, it is also soul-damaging.

Man's law is enforced by government officers. Sentence passed on the convicted is frequently based upon incomplete evidence. But God's law is enforced or substantiated by man's own conscience, by God's direct redeeming intervention, and by the natural outworking of the laws of cause and effect. Man's law can only deter crime, but God's law inspires virtue. In God's court there is perfect justice. Here the attorney-at-law would have no advantage over the illiterate, for each is convicted by his conscience and judged by his own inward law—the internal law of God's love and grace. Only an Omnipresent and Omniscient God can qualify as the judge, for He alone can discern the true motive of each action.

Our acceptance with God is already secure in Jesus Christ. "Ye are complete in him."[4] What the Father thinks of Christ makes us acceptable to God, in Jesus. Let us remember that this inward law is implanted by God when we accept "Jesus only" as our righteousness. By the power of the Holy Spirit, bringing resurrection power into our lives—as the same power by which Jesus rose from the dead—the inward law becomes the motivation for and direction of our lives. In essence it is the implanting of the Ten Commandments in the wellsprings of our thoughts and actions.

When written in human hearts, God's law becomes their inward law. The spirit, rather than the letter of the law, is the focus of attention. It takes more than blind obedience to be a keeper of such a law. A willingness to accept this law, a realization of one's inability to satisfy its demands, and a faith in Christ—who has fulfilled the law perfectly *for us* and who now fulfills the law *in us* by divinely endowed power—become the secret of victory over sin by the remnant who "keep the commandments of God, and have the testimony of Jesus Christ."[5]

1. Jeremiah 31:33
2. Judges 21:25
3. James 1:25
4. Colossians 2:10
5. Revelation 12:17

Love—The Supreme Motive

Once Jesus reduced the commandments to just two points: "love the Lord thy God with all thy heart, and with all thy soul, and with all thy mind," and "love thy neighbour as thyself."[1] To reduce the commandments even further, we could describe God's law in one word: Love. The beloved disciple John said, "God is love,"[2] and the apostle Paul proclaimed, Now abide faith, hope, love, these three; but the greatest of these is love."[3]

Love is an emotion, but not merely an emotion—it is a principle. We find meaning in life because we know somebody loves us. We are enabled to truly do good because we love. Yet we are all sinful and selfish. And when the love of self becomes dominant, we forget the welfare of others. One may become so blind to the needs of others that he pursues his own goals regardless of whether doing so causes pain or even death to others. If everyone on earth were to become totally and unfailingly selfish and exceedingly ruthless in pursuing his own goals, law enforcement on earth would break down. Violence would rule.

As there is no darkness in light, there is no selfishness in love. The Bible tells us that in love there is no boastfulness, hypocrisy, jealousy, envy, pride, rudeness, irritability, grudge bearing, or failure.[4] "There is no fear in love; but perfect love casteth out fear; because fear hath torment. He that feareth is not made perfect in love."[5] Love "shall cover the multitude of sins."[6]

True love changes not and endures forever. We must thank God that He has this kind of love for us. Had He not, we would have been forsaken when we rebelled and stumbled. The love of a father or mother goes out to the prodigal son who wanders from home to live a sinful life. Our heavenly Father's love can draw us to Him as a magnet draws the compass needle.

Christ loves us exceedingly. And in continuing to love us, He also has great faith and great hope in us. Only when we turn to look with faith into the face of Christ—the Christ on the cross—will our hearts be touched by this matchless love and will we surrender ourselves unconditionally to Him. We will find that although we are entirely undeserving, we cannot turn down His great love—love that we can neither fully describe nor understand.

"Love is patient, love is kind." "Love does not delight in evil but rejoices with the truth. It always protects, always trusts, always hopes, always preserves."[7]

From these verses we learn that love includes patience, kindness, truthfulness, faith, and hope. Love without patience is not enduring love. Love is expressed in kindness. Love rejoices not over wrong but over truth. Love without faith results in suspicion and jealousy. And love without hope would bring emptiness and frustration. Love involves all these factors together.

Love is something which most of us have experienced, but none of us fully understands. We cannot live meaningfully without love. Our lives are sustained by it. Yet sinful men are selfish and full of hatred—the opposite of love. To say what love is not may be easier than to say what love is, because we see far more selfishness and hatred around us than we see love.

Love is altruistic. Love is giving of self to another, sharing something with him. But the greatest love is that seen in the life of Christ, who made the supreme sacrifice for sinners even before they knew Him, even when they hated Him. Such love does not originate on this earth; it is divine.

"When love fills the heart, it will flow out to others, not because of favors received from them, but because love is the principle of action. Love modifies the character, governs the impulses, subdues enmity, and ennobles the affections. This love is as broad as the universe, and is in harmony with that of the angel workers."[8]

"Love's agencies have wonderful power, for they are divine. The soft answer that 'turneth away wrath,' the love that 'suffereth long, and is kind,' the charity that 'covereth a multitude of sins' (Proverbs 15:1; 1 Corinthians 13:4, R.V.; 1 Peter 4:8, R.V.)—would we learn the lesson, with what power for healing would our lives be gifted! How life would be transformed, and the earth become a very likeness and foretaste of heaven!"[9]

Love "does not envy, it does not boast, it is not proud. It is not rude, it is not self-seeking, it is not easily angered, it keeps no record of wrongs. Love does not delight in evil."[10]

Looking at love from another angle, we notice that the Bible does list what love is not: (1) envy, (2) boastfulness, (3) arrogance and rudeness, (4) self-seeking, (5) irritability, (6) resentfulness, and (7) the disposition to rejoice over wrong. All of these things are negative factors which are harmful to one's personality and to human relations.

When a Christian is jealous of others and intolerant of their feelings, he brings dishonor upon the Christian name. We do not win others by bluntly telling them of their weaknesses or by condemning their wrong actions. If we have love that is long-suffering and kind, we will have a tender spirit, a gentle and winning way that will save and build.

True love is not sentimentalism or a selfish, lustful feeling. True love is not temporary; it endures changes of time and circumstance. Love is a principle; it does not change. Love means sharing, giving, and sacrificing. A mother's love is great, a woman's love is deep, a friend's love—like Jonathan's toward David—may be deeply moving: but only God's love is everlasting. And God's love is more wonderful than anything else we may experience or understand.

Without love, all virtue becomes hollow. Speaking with the tongues of men and angels, having the gift of prophecy, understanding all mysteries and all knowledge, and giving everything to the poor are good deeds. But they are not truly good if the motive behind them is selfish. Love must be the motive for all good work. Only love can keep one doing good continually regardless of what others feel and do. To help to serve, to donate if done for fame or for pleasure, cannot be sustained for long. Love and love alone endures forever.

"Love never fails. But where there are prophecies, they will cease; where there are tongues they will be stilled; where there is knowledge, it will pass away."[11] This verse focuses on the time element. Nothing in this world can be called everlasting. Almost all things last but a short while and then pass away. Empires, pyramids, great walls, skyscrapers, things made by human hands will pass away. Heroes, kings, and scholars will also pass away and be forgotten. Of all things human, only love lasts forever. Since only that which is living is capable of loving, we must first have eternal life before we can love forever.

Timeless love means love which can endure trial, tribulation, and even denial. Paul, touched by the measureless love of Jesus, cried out, "Who shall separate us from the love of Christ? shall tribulation, or distress, or persecution, or famine, or nakedness, or peril, or sword?"[12] While their intentions may be admirable, how many Christians would be able to endure the trials Paul did and still be loyal to Christ? But Jesus' love is timeless and changeless.

"The divine Teacher bears with the erring through all their perversity. His love does not grow cold; His efforts to win them do not cease. With outstretched arms He waits to welcome again and again the erring, the rebellious, and even the apostate. His heart is touched with the helplessness of the little child subject to rough usage. The cry of human suffering never reaches His ear in vain. Though all are precious in His sight, the rough, sullen, stubborn dispositions draw most heavily upon His sympathy and love; for He traces from cause to effect. The one who is most easily tempted, and is most inclined to err, is the special object of His solicitude."[13]

In the life to come, the corruptible nature is changed forever. Yet even now, in Christ, the imperfect becomes more perfect, more complete; the selfish becomes more selfless. God takes away our selfish, stony hearts and gives us hearts of flesh—tender, compassionate, capable of loving. This miracle can only be wrought when we submit ourselves *totally* to Christ.

To go to an enemy and say "I'm sorry" takes courage. Only the grace of God can help us love our enemies, but we may learn to love as Christ loves.

We take for granted that we usually love the members of our families more than friends, and friends more than strangers. But in heaven there will be no strangers. Our capacity to love will increase so that we will treat everyone alike.

Some Christians say that they must live with their mothers, or wives, or children in heaven—that if they cannot live with them, heaven will not mean anything. This feeling is based on imperfect knowledge and imperfect love. Jesus Christ once said, "In the resurrection they neither marry, nor are given in marriage, but are as the angels of God in heaven."[14]

Here Jesus pulls aside the curtain of mystery and allows us to see a glimpse of heaven. There our imperfect love will be perfect. Human relations will broaden and take different forms. We just cannot use the small yardstick of this earth to measure the love of heaven.

"Since there is no fear in love, one who fears demonstrates that he is not yet made perfect in respect to the high form of love of which the apostle is speaking. Fortunately, development is possible. As we learn to know the Lord we begin to love Him, and our fear changes from a haunting dread of a powerful and avenging God to a 'clean' (Ps. 19:9) fear that does not wish to disappoint a friend."[15]

"These three remain: faith, hope and love. But the greatest of these is love."[16] Though we need not worry now about what the psychology or sociology of heaven will be, we must learn here and now to grow in love daily—to grow more like Jesus. On this earth, where we see things as though looking through darkened glass, we must have faith. With eyes of faith we see beyond the glass to peace and confidence in the future.

We must also have hope. Without hope our eyes would be fixed on the present and the past, and the memory of unpleasant things might seem unbearable. But with hope, we can endure all kinds of hardship and be patient until we reach our goal. When we see Jesus face-to-face, we will no longer need faith; neither will we need hope, because we will have arrived in what is now the future—infinite time. Yet love abides forever—in the past, the present, and the future—even in heaven eternal. To have strong faith is admirable, yet how much more we need to have strong love!

We need to hold fast our hope—the blessed hope—of the return of Christ. But only His strong love for us and our love for Him can carry us through the most difficult trials and temptations, that we may not lose our hope. What we Laodiceans lack today is not more money. We are counseled to buy gold tried in the fire, white raiment, and eyesalve that we may have riches, clothing and sight. Our lukewarmness as Laodiceans is caused by our love for earthly things. Because of this, many have already turned away and are no longer on the pilgrimage to God's kingdom. Let us learn to love God, to love each other, and to love strangers—even enemies—that we may truly be called sons and daughters of God.

"The divine love emanating from Christ never destroys human love, but includes it. By it human love is refined and purified, elevated and ennobled. Human love can never bear its precious fruit until it is united with the divine nature and trained to grow heavenward."[17]

In summary, God's law is love. God is prepared to write His love in our hearts as the inward law. He has even promised that our stony hearts, which are incapable of responding to His love, will be taken away. Then He will give us hearts of flesh that we may respond to His love with love and learn to love others as He does.

We all like to be loved. But in order to be loved by others, we must love them first. God has loved us first, and now He tells us to love one another. Let us accept this great gift of love that it may permeate all our motives, train our consciences, and become the inward law which governs all our actions so that we may truly be like Him.

"Behold, what manner of love the Father hath bestowed upon us, that we should be called the sons of God. . . . Beloved, now are we the sons of God, and it doth not yet appear what we shall be: but we know that, when he shall appear, we shall be like him; for we shall see him as he is. And every man that hath this hope in him purifieth himself, even as he is pure."[18]

1. Matthew 22:37, 39.
2. 1 John 4:8.
3. 1 Corinthians 13:13, NASB.
4. 1 Corinthians 13.
5. 1 John 4:18.
6. 1 Peter 4:8. Also see Proverbs 10:12.
7. 1 Corinthians 13:4, 6, 7, NIV.
8. Ellen G. White, *Thoughts From the Mount of Blessing*, p. 38.
9. Ellen G. White, *Education*, p. 114.
10. 1 Corinthians 13:4-6, NIV.
11. 1 Corinthians 13:8.
12. Romans 8:35.
13. Ellen G. White, *Education*, p. 294.
14. Matthew 22:30.
15. *S.D.A. Bible Commentary*, vol. 7, p. 670.
16. 1 Corinthians 13:13, NIV.
17. Ellen G. White, *The Adventist Home*, p. 99.
18. 1 John 3:1-3.

Conscience—Voice of the Spirit

The ability to discern between right and wrong was given to man when God created him. What is considered as right may differ from culture to culture, from time to time, and from place to place. But the ability to separate right from wrong—a gift received at creation—has not been completely lost under the influence of sin. Nor have millennia of physical, mental, and moral degeneration entirely destroyed this faculty of the mind—the conscience.

Webster's New World Dictionary defines conscience as "a knowledge or feeling of right and wrong, with a compulsion to do right; moral judgment that prohibits or opposes the violation of a previously recognized ethical principle."

The *S.D.A. Bible Dictionary* gives an even better definition: conscience is a "moral consciousness, . . . an inward faculty of consciousness that sits in judgment on the moral rightness of thoughts, words, and actions, independent of the individual's desires or inclinations."[1]

The Bible speaks of a good conscience,[2] a pure conscience,[3] and a conscience void of offense toward God.[4] It also talks about a weak conscience,[5] a conscience that can be defiled,[6] seared with a hot iron,[7] or put away.[8] Fortunately, the Bible also teaches that the conscience can be cleansed and purged.[9] The shed blood of the Saviour speaks sensitivity to the conscience. In much greater detail, the spirit of prophecy describes a conscience which, when quickened by the Holy Spirit, can become a safe guide for our conduct.

The Lord has promised that "thine ears shall hear a word behind thee, saying, This is the way, walk ye in it, when ye turn to the right hand and when ye turn to the left."[10]

We make decisions every day, some routine and some more important. Everyone is forced to make serious decisions many times in his lifetime. Often, because the future is unknown, decision-making becomes an agonizing experience. A choice may mean success or failure, even life or death. "How should I decide?" or "What should I choose?" are questions many people ask every day. Sometimes even when faced by the not-so-serious decisions, we wish someone would point out the right way. Fortunately, we do have such help made available to us by a loving God. He has created a conscience in our minds so that we hear an inner voice which tells us what is right and what is wrong. Those believing in Christ and His Word know that this is the voice of the Holy Spirit. If we yield ourselves to this voice, the sweet influence of the Holy Spirit will lead us and transform us.

"Not by eloquence or logic are men's hearts reached, but by the sweet influences of the Holy Spirit, which operate quietly yet surely in transforming and developing character. It is the still, small voice of the Spirit of God that has power to change the heart."[11]

"The spirit of truth and a good conscience are sufficient to inspire and regulate the motives and conduct of those who learn of Christ and are like Him."[12]

Though the conscience is the faculty which differentiates right from wrong, the sense of what is right may differ from person to person because not all people permit the conscience to be educated and controlled by the Holy Spirit. Only the Holy Spirit can quicken the mind and help a person unfailingly discern the highest ethical standards as established by God. Through the study of the Bible and through prayer, we understand God's will, His law, and His expectations in Christian behavior. But when we are confronted with difficult decisions, neither our learning nor our conscience is a sufficiently dependable guide. We need to rely upon the Holy Spirit to help us uphold God's law and behave according to His standard.

"The renewing, sanctifying influence of the Holy Spirit, which would give peace and hope to the troubled conscience, and restore health and happiness to the soul,"[13] is the only sure guide for the conscience.

Jesus said, "When the Comforter is come, whom I will send unto you from the Father, even the Spirit of truth, which proceedeth from the Father, he shall testify of me."[14] In order to really know Christ and to understand the Bible, we need the Holy Spirit. Only through the influence of the Holy Spirit can we come to know Jesus.

The conscience, if not carefully guarded, can virtually be destroyed. "It is true that some may see their folly and repent. God may pardon them. But they have wounded their own souls, and brought upon themselves a lifelong peril. The power of discernment, which ought ever to be kept keen and sensitive to distinguish between right and wrong, is in a great measure destroyed. They are not quick to recognize the guiding voice of the Holy Spirit, or to discern the devices of Satan. Too often in time of danger they fall under temptation, and are led away from God. The end of their pleasure-loving life is ruin for this world and for the world to come."[15]

God, in His great mercy, has provided a guide for our footsteps—a conscience that is at work not only in the hearts of those who believe in Him but also in the hearts of those who may not understand His law; for God has no favorites.[16] If unbelievers do not have a conscience, the Holy Spirit cannot influence them, and their conversion is not possible. That non-Christians may become Christians testifies to the fact that the conscience is a gift God has given to every human being.

"For when the Gentiles, which have not the law, do by nature the things contained in the law, these, having not the law, are a law unto themselves: which shew the work of the law written in their hearts, their conscience also bearing witness, and their thoughts the mean while accusing or else excusing one another."[17]

"If you cherish a habitual impression that God sees and hears all that you do and say, and keeps a faithful record of all your words and actions, and that you must meet it all, then in all you do and say you will seek to follow the dictates of an enlightened and wakeful conscience."[18]

In this world, many people are not sure of themselves, having never learned to think for themselves. They constantly need suggestions or directions from others to help them make decisions. If they do not come to God for wisdom and guidance, their minds may ultimately be controlled by others.

"In the kingdoms of the world, position meant self-aggrandizement. The people were supposed to exist for the benefit of the ruling classes. Influence, wealth, education, were so many means of gaining control of the masses for the use of the leaders. The higher classes were to think, decide, enjoy, and rule; the lower were to obey and serve. Religion, like all things else, was a matter of authority. The people were expected to believe and practice as their superiors directed. The right of man as man, to think and act for himself, was wholly unrecognized."[19]

Church leaders, parents, teachers, dormitory deans, husbands and wives, brothers and sisters, psychologists and psychiatrists, work supervisors, pastors, counselors, evangelists, and Bible instructors—all of these and many others need constantly to be alert to the danger of being conscience for another, especially when the other may invite it.

But "God never designed that one human mind should be under the complete control of another. And those who make efforts to have the individuality of their pupils merged in themselves, and to be mind, will, and conscience for them assume fearful responsibilities."[20]

The conscience is tender and sensitive and can be

severely impaired. "A conscience once violated is greatly weakened. It needs the strength of constant watchfulness and unceasing prayer. You are standing in a slippery place. You need all the strength that the truth can give to fortify you and save you from making entire shipwreck. Life and death are before you; which will you choose?"[21]

Saying No to an enlightened conscience is the surest way to weaken its effectiveness. Like an alarm clock repeatedly turned off before the sleeper actually arises, the voice of conscience is heard less and less. Ultimately it will be deadened and lose its soul-protecting power. Even in the work of God it is possible for the road of progress to be blocked when those in responsible positions have perverted the conscience to the point that it is hard and unimpressible.

The youth also need to keep the conscience tender and instructed by Spirit-directed Bible study. To those young people whose conscience is slumbering, the Lord speaks these words: "If you could only arouse, if your slumbering, deadened conscience could be awakened, and you could cherish a habitual impression of the presence of God, and keep yourself subject to the control of an enlightened, wakeful conscience, you would be happy yourself and a blessing to your parents, whose hearts you now wound."[22]

Young people who have received religious instruction at home and who go away—comparatively innocent and virtuous to schools or jobs—may become corrupt by seeking the company of worldly minded people. In the process, they lose self-respect and sacrifice noble principles. Little remains to keep them from the downward path, for they have rejected their conscience to the place where sin does not appear so sinful anymore.

Repeatedly in the Scriptures and in helpful comments on them the message comes through that the sensitivity of the conscience is affected by what an individual does or shrinks from doing. Shunning the cross weakens conviction as to future duties, and soon disobedience fails to disturb the soul. Only a continual love-response to Calvary's all-sufficient Sacrifice can keep the heart tender to Spirit-directed duty. Otherwise "the heart is hardened, the conscience seared."[23]

Conscience is not only an inner voice, a sixth sense; it is the most important part of the decision-making mechanism. Through the conscience the Holy Spirit directs the will and controls the whole life. When violated, the sensitivity of the conscience can be so blunted and benumbed that one does not see sin as sin. Therefore, God, in His great love, promises to take out the stony heart and put within man a heart of flesh which can respond to the voice of the Holy Spirit. Only with such a new heart and a new spirit can one walk in His statutes and keep his commandments.[24]

If one does not rely upon help from the Holy Spirit but allows his conscience to be silenced, he commits the unpardonable sin. It is so easy to fall into the trap which caught the boy who called, "Wolf! Wolf!" when there was no wolf. When there actually was a wolf, his fearful cries brought him no help. He had played his game too long. With regard to the conscience, we may, instead of shouting, habitually silence the warning voice, but with similar results in the end.

"Those who are quieting a guilty conscience with the thought that they can change a course of evil when they choose, that they can trifle with the invitations of mercy, and yet be again and again impressed, take this course at their peril. They think that after casting all their influence on the side of the great rebel, in a moment of utmost extremity, when danger compasses them about, they will change leaders. But this is not so easily done. The experience, the education, the discipline of a life of sinful indulgence, has so thoroughly molded the character that they cannot then receive the image of Jesus. Had no light shone upon their pathway, the case would have been different. Mercy might interpose, and give them an opportunity to accept her overtures; but after light has been long rejected and despised, it will be finally withdrawn."[25]

"By continuing their course of sin, they are violating

their consciences, hardening their hearts, and stiffening their necks, just the same as though the testimony had been borne directly to them. In passing on and refusing to put away their sins and correct their wrongs by humble confession, repentance, and humiliations, they choose their own way, and are given up to the same, and are finally led captive by Satan at his will."[26]

"It is by the Spirit that God works upon the heart; when men willfully reject the Spirit, and declare It to be from Satan, they cut off the channel by which God can communicate with them. When the Spirit is finally rejected, there is no more that God can do for the soul."[27]

The problem of a seared conscience does have a solution. Mentioned earlier, it bears repeating, lest some become tempted to give up in despair. The feeblest positive response to the voice of the Spirit-directed conscience will open the way for Christ's grace to enter the soul for redemption. As a physically sick person can regain strength by carefully planned exercise—even if it be simple at first—so the spiritually sick can receive remarkable results by exercising faith in the mercy of Christ. Even the smallest measure of faith can bring from God warmth, love, understanding, an illuminated conscience, and a will responsive to the Spirit's prompting.[28]

"Yield yourself to Christ without delay; He alone, by the power of His grace, can redeem you from ruin. He alone can bring your moral and mental powers into a state of health. Your heart may be warm with the love of God; your understanding, clear and mature; your conscience, illuminated, quick, and pure; your will, upright and sanctified, subject to the control of the Spirit of God."[29]

1. *S.D.A. Bible Dictionary*, p. 220.
2. 1 Timothy 1:5.
3. 1 Timothy 3:9.
4. Acts 24:16.
5. 1 Corinthians 8:10, 12.
6. Titus 1:15.
7. 1 Timothy 4:2.
8. 1 Timothy 1:19.

9. Hebrews 9:14.
10. Isaiah 30:21.
11. Ellen G. White, *Prophets and Kings*, p. 169.
12. Ellen G. White, *Testimonies*, vol. 2, p. 487.
13. Ellen G. White, *Testimonies*, Vol. 3, p. 186.
14. John 15:26.
15. Ellen G. White, *Christ's Object Lessons*, p. 55.
16. See Acts 10:34.
17. Romans 2:14, 15.
18. Ellen G. White, *Testimonies*, vol. 4, p. 244.
19. Ellen G. White, *The Desire of Ages*, p. 550.
20. Ellen G. White, *Testimonies*, vol. 3, p. 134.
21. Ellen G. White, *Testimonies*, vol. 2, pp. 90, 91.
22. Ellen G. White, *Testimonies*, vol. 2, p. 563.
23. Ellen G. White, *Christ's Object Lessons*, p. 279.
24. See Ezekiel 11:19, 20.
25. Ellen G. White, *Patriarchs and Prophets*, p. 269.
26. Ellen G. White, *Testimonies*, vol. 2, pp. 447, 448.
27. Ellen G. White, *The Desire of Ages*, p. 322.
28. See Mark 9:24 and context.
29. Ellen G. White, *Testimonies*, vol. 2, pp. 564, 565.

Developing a Personal Moral Standard

What is considered good in one place or at one time may be considered bad in another location or time. Therefore the sense of good and bad—a person's value system—is largely subjective and molded by cultural background.

Two hundred years ago, doctors used bleeding as a therapy for reducing fevers. This was considered good for the body. Today it would be unthinkable for a doctor to bleed a patient in order to heal him.

Until about ten years ago, many people in the Orient thought that lard was very nutritious. But now these same people insist on using only corn oil—no animal fats. What was considered good has become bad!

While these examples are clear-cut and easily understood, other situations may illustrate other views of morality. In some places, society in general still considers passing money under the table as a necessary—if not even advisable—means of getting things done faster and better. Even though the law against corruption is clear, many feel that such a law is unreasonable and unnecessary. Thus they keep on doing what they feel necessary and even "good," arguing that passing a little money under the table differs little from giving tips to the taxi driver or the waitress in a restaurant. If these small tips are permitted by the government, so they reason, why should bigger "tips" be labeled "corruption?"

Some Catholics may apparently agree with the pope

that abortion is wrong. Yet they do not refrain from the use of contraceptive devices, which is also definitely against the pope's will. They may conclude that while it is good not to kill, it is maybe even better to prevent life in the first place.

Such standards and styles as skirt length for women, necktie width for men, or hair length for both sexes vary from time to time. If a salesman tried to sell you something not in fashion, you might think he was cheating you or treating you as a hillbilly. A sense of the appropriateness of a certain standard may vary from person to person.

A scribe once asked Jesus this question: "Good Master, what good thing shall I do, that I may have eternal life?" Jesus answered by asking a question in return—"Why callest thou me good? there is none good but one, that is, God: but if thou wilt enter into life, keep the commandments."[1]

Jesus proclaims here a standard for measuring goodness that transcends all personal and subjective judgment. God is the source of all that is good. He is the sum total of wisdom. He is love, and He is the Creator. That wisdom, love, and divine creative power are good is true regardless of any individual understanding of what is good.

"Goodness is the result of divine power transforming human nature. By believing in Christ, the fallen race He has redeemed may obtain that faith which works by love and purifies the soul from all defilement."[2]

But to British moral philosopher G. E. Moore, goodness is impossible to define, since it is the designation of a simple, inscrutable characteristic of things. Even though we may judge some things to be good, we cannot prove that they are good. They are good in our eyes because we think they are good. Goodness—apart from that set forth by God—is a subjective concept. That is why what is considered good differs from person to person.

Most moral philosophers refuse to commit themselves to any moral code. When one refuses to accept an absolute, eternal, and unchangeable moral standard and believes instead in a standard of right and wrong dependent on circumstances of time and place, he will soon find himself totally adrift. When one eliminates God from his system of thought and tries to construct for himself a set of moral standards, he produces only trifling and limited statements, which stand dwarfed before the broad, majestic, and beautiful truths stated in the Bible.

As early as about 300 B.C., the matter of whether man is basically good or bad was debated by two great Confucianist scholars—Mencius and Shuntze. (Hsün-tzu). Of course, the debate came to no satisfactory conclusion, for man is neither wholly good nor wholly bad.

Aristotle, the Greek philosopher, states in his book *Ethics* that every reasoned human activity aims at some good. But unlike Plato, he saw that there cannot be a universal good, since goodness, in the human eye, is a value based only on personal opinion.

Measured by his own standard, one may pronounce himself good. But that good may not stand the test of some other standard of goodness. Only God's standard is the real and unchanging rule—the standard which can be applied to all.

Today men are acting as in the days of the judges, when "every man did that which was right in his own eyes."[3] Will such ever see that they are wrong? Sinners "will find in the day of judgment that they turned from God's express requirements and set up their own opinion as a standard of right and wrong. They will find that what seemed to them unimportant was not so regarded of God. His requirements should be sacredly obeyed."[4]

Here on earth, what is considered right or wrong is often relative. As one writer suggests, law is essentially an aspect of culture. Man's concepts of right or wrong are largely nurtured by cultural background. Law regulates behavior and sets limits on what ought or ought not to be done. As a major instrument of social control, the law of the land rewards or penalizes behavior. In order to enforce a law, society values a sense of honor and sanctions a contract agreed to by two or more parties. Physical force is sometimes used as a last resort.

Because circumstances and cultures differ, human law is somewhat relative. For example, in severe cold weather, when food supplies are low, permitting infants or the aged to die is acceptable among some peoples. The aged may deliberately walk out into a blizzard or into the desert. In other cultures, such behavior would not be tolerated.

As patterns of behavior permitted by law may differ widely, so may standards of goodness unless based on divine law and instruction. What is *legally* right may differ from what is *morally* right. In the eyes of legislators, a law can be a good law or a bad law. But once a law is enacted, violation of even a bad law is never legally right; for the very function of law is to point out what has been defined as crime. In the eyes of a judge, all laws must be enforced and respected, whether good or bad. The Christian may at times find himself unable to fully harmonize with what is defined as legal because of his allegiance to a higher law.

Each person and each group has a set of inward laws which may have been molded by culture, education, socioeconomic status, occupation, age, location, religion, and other factors. Since such humanly derived inward laws are changeable, relative, and subjective, God wants to write His own law—a much higher and moral standard, the expression of His character—in our hearts. His law transcends culture, race, age, class, religion, time, and locality. He invites us to accept it in place of our imperfect, incomplete, and defective moral concepts. God urges us to accept His law as a covenant. By accepting it, we will be His people and He will be our God.

"As man yields to temptation, and indulges in sin, his mind becomes darkened. The moral sense is perverted. The warnings of conscience are disregarded, and its voice is less clearly heard. He gradually loses the power to distinguish between right and wrong, until he has no true sense of his standing before God. He may observe the forms of religion and zealously maintain its doctrines, while destitute of its spirit."[5]

In the book of Romans, the apostle Paul vividly described the battle going on in his heart: "That which I do I allow not: for what I would, that do I not; but what I hate, that do I. . . . Now then it is no more I that do it, but sin that dwelleth in me. . . . For the good that I would I do not: but the evil which I would not, that I do." "But I see another law in my members, warring against the law of my mind, and bringing me into captivity to the law of sin which is in my members."[6]

If we look at this situation from a legal viewpoint, we find no solution to the problems of inner battle or a guilty conscience. Only by looking into the face of Jesus can we receive in Him the power to choose and do what is right. His love can melt all the ice in our hearts and win all arguments against yielding to sin.

The heart that has been converted by the love of God revealed at Calvary *cannot* treat lightly the will of God in any sphere in life. "Whenever one renounces sin, which is the transgression of the law, his life will be brought into conformity to the law, into perfect obedience. This is the work of the Holy Spirit. The light of the word carefully studied, the voice of conscience, the strivings of the Spirit, produce in the heart genuine love for Christ, who gave Himself a whole sacrifice to redeem the whole person, body, soul, and spirit. And love is manifested in obedience."[7]

The law written by God on tables of stone is written by the Holy Spirit upon the tables of the heart. We may have perpetual peace of mind in knowing that, rather than seeking to establish our own righteousness, we may accept the righteousness of Christ. His blood atones for our sins. Pardon is free to all. At the same time, the heart renewed by the Holy Spirit will bring forth "the fruit of the Spirit."[8] Through the grace of Christ we shall live in obedience to the inward law—the law of God written upon our hearts.

We develop a character which is the counterpart of

the divine character. Growing into His likeness, we enlarge our capacity for knowing God. More and more we enter into fellowship with the heavenly world, and we have continually increasing power to receive the riches of the knowledge and wisdom of eternity."[9]

Not without conscious effort on our part do our lives come to resemble more and more the divine Pattern. Truth must be brought into the everyday life and made practical. The Christian life is not a dreamlike drift toward the kingdom of heaven. It involves choices, decisions, goals. It involves conscious denial of the ever-present demands of fashion, custom, and the teachings and practices of the world.

As a relentless tide of worldly influences repeatedly sweeps against us, we must have the quality of solid rock in our characters to remain unmoved by it all. Looking ever to the cross of Jesus, we will have moral courage to shun the customs of the world while remaining open to the heart needs of our fellowmen.

"Desires for goodness and true holiness are right so far as they go; but if you stop here, they will avail nothing. Good purposes are right, but will prove of no avail unless resolutely carried out. Many will be lost while hoping and desiring to be Christians; but they made no earnest effort, therefore they will be weighed in the balances and found wanting. The will must be exercised in the right direction."[10]

Practically all cultures place good above bad. When one reaches for good, he reaches upward. The Christian recognizes the upward reach as the Godward reach. How appropriate that every impulse for good originates with God, the source of all goodness.

Christ has the means and power to lead His children to wholehearted moral and spiritual soundness. He can feed us leaves from the tree of life as we study His Word. He can draw us to His throne of grace and put a prayer in our hearts that will bring just the needed help. He will make available all the resources of heaven to the heart that senses its need. We "are complete in him."[11]

1. Matthew 19:15, 17.
2. Ellen G. White, *My Life Today*, p. 54.
3. Judges 21:25.
4. Ellen G. White, *Counsels on Health*, p. 70.
5. Ellen G. White, *Testimonies*, vol. 5, p. 682.
6. Romans 7:15-19, 23.
7. Ellen G. White, *Testimonies*, vol. 6, p. 92.
8. See Galatians 5:22, 23.
9. Ellen G. White, *Christ's Object Lessons*, p. 355.
10. Ellen G. White, *Testimonies*, vol. 2, pp. 265, 266.
11. Colossians 2:10.

Freedom of Choice

Along with a conscience, God gives man freedom of choice. One may choose to believe in God, choose not to believe in any god, or actually create a god for oneself. One may choose to marry a Margaret or a Karen, a Peter or a John. Even trivial things, one still has to make choices—a salad or a sandwich, an apple or a mango.

When we choose something, we must take into account the limits and consequences of the choice. The apostle Paul wrote that even though he was free to do lawful things, he would not allow his liberty to become a stumbling block to others weak in faith. So we find that a Christian does not have complete freedom.

Difficult choices may confront us. A judge, in sentencing a minor offender, must weigh the safety of society at large against the future of the defendant. A doctor has to decide which patient shall benefit when life-saving equipment is in short supply. Parents often have to decide whether they should discipline their child, how and when. All these people have freedom of choice, yet their freedom is clearly limited.

The most serious choice each of us must make is like that of Christ in Gethsemane—the choice as to whether we will wholeheartedly dedicate everything we have and are to God. Some may feel that they can surrender only partially to God now, planning that at some point in the future they will decide to serve God without reservation. Thus they hope to gain all the advantages of this world and also of heaven. But they may suddenly die, and eternal life will forever be lost to them. Unless, "looking unto Jesus," we put everything on the altar, unless we decide that to please God is our highest goal in life, it is so easy to falter.

Unfortunately, some dedicate all they have to a task, an ideal, or a goal, but not to God. When these tasks or ideals take the place of God, they become idols—idols of money, fame, position, power, ideology, beauty, education, or possessions.

The drive to build a hospital, a new building for a college, or even a church can crowd God out. A church building project may become an idol. If we are not careful, some idolatrous "graven image" may take the place in our minds which should be reserved for God alone.

"No outward shrines may be visible, there may be no image for the eye to rest upon, yet we may be practicing idolatry. It is as easy to make an idol of cherished ideas or objects as to fashion gods of wood or stone. Thousands have a false conception of God and His attributes. They are as verily serving a false god as were the servants of Baal."[1]

"And a certain ruler asked him, saying, Good Master, what shall I do to inherit eternal life? And Jesus said unto him, Why callest thou me good? none is good, save one, that is, God. Thou knowest the commandments, Do not commit adultery, Do not kill, Do not steal, Do not bear false witness, Honour thy father and thy mother. And he said, All these have I kept from my youth up. Now when Jesus heard these things, he said unto him, Yet lackest thou one thing: sell all that thou hast, and distribute unto the poor, and thou shalt have treasure in heaven: and come, follow me. And when he heard this, he was very sorrowful: for he was very rich. And when Jesus saw that he was very sorrowful, he said, How hardly shall they that have riches enter into the kingdom of God! For it is easier for a camel to go through a needle's eye, than for a rich man to enter into the kingdom of God. And they that heard it said, Who then can be saved? And he said, The things which are impossible with men are possible with God."[2]

"He [the young ruler] had cherished an idol in the soul; the world was his god. He professed to have kept the commandments, but he was destitute of the principle which is the very spirit of life of them all. He did not possess true love for God or man."[3]

An endless battle is waged for the affections of the followers of Jesus Christ. When our love for Him grows cold and feeble, the world surges in with its earthly treasures as an enticement for our attention. Only as we consciously choose to expel these potential idols from our hearts will our love for Christ revive.

"When one idol is expelled from the soul, Satan has another prepared to supply its place. Unless you make an entire consecration to Christ and live in communion with Him, unless you make Him your Counselor, you will find that your heart, open to evil thoughts, is easily diverted from the service of God to the service of self."[4]

God is a jealous God. Having given His Son to die in order to restore our lost eternal life, He expects our total loyalty. Since His love for us is total, a halfhearted dedication on our part is unacceptable to Him. In a certain sense, the first three commandments tell us only one thing—love God with an undivided heart. God must be placed at the highest level of our hierarchy of needs or values.

Jesus is our perfect Model and Pattern. The only purpose of His life was to do the Father's will and to glorify Him. If we would only focus our attention on Christ—His life, His sacrifice, His intercession—and learn His life-style, we would have no other gods. We would cherish no idols in our hearts. We would utter no words to bring shame to His name. We would do nothing to misrepresent His character. When self becomes unimportant and God all-important, God's law of love will liberate us; and Satan will be unable to plant an idol in our hearts.

Paul once wrote: "If any of them that believe not bid you to a feast, and ye be disposed to go; whatsoever is set before you, eat, asking no question for conscience sake. But if any man say unto you, This is offered in sacrifice unto idols, eat not for his sake that shewed it, and for conscience sake: for the earth is the Lord's, and the fulness thereof: conscience, I say, not thine own, but of the other: for why is my liberty judged of another man's conscience?''[5]

Paul is not here concerned with the question of whether or not meat is a wholesome food to eat. The subject is that of meat offered to idols. The lesson is one of personal and religious freedom. Everyone likes freedom, and some want unlimited freedom. But the apostle Paul felt differently. He would not use his liberty in such a way that doubt was created in the minds of others. We are all free to make choices, but we are not free to choose just whatever we like. Our choices must be guided by a set of mature inward laws.

Some Christians have stronger faith, and some have weaker faith. A frank and testing statement may stimulate one to study his Bible more, but the same may result in doubts in the mind of another. Mature Christians must be considerate of the needs and weaknesses of others.

"Take heed lest by any means this liberty of your's become a stumblingblock to them that are weak. For if any man see thee which hast knowledge sit at meat in the idol's temple, shall not the conscience of him which is weak be emboldened to eat those things which are offered to idols; and through thy knowledge shall the weak brother perish, for whom Christ died?''[6]

In Paul's day, the offering of food to idols did not change its nutritional value (and he was not here teaching about a better diet). But the apostle would refrain from eating such food for the sake of those with a weak conscience. Likewise, Christians today should also be careful lest without wishing it, they cause a weak fellow Christian to stumble.

"By some, all efforts to establish order are regarded as dangerous—as a restriction of personal liberty, and hence to be feared as popery. These deceived souls regard it a virtue to boast of their freedom to think and act independently. . . . I have been instructed that it is

Satan's special effort to lead men to feel that God is pleased to have them choose their own course independent of the counsel of their brethren."[7]

Seventh-day Adventists are very conscious of religious freedom and are perpetual "watchdogs" over those whom they fear may be planning to restrict their liberties. But Paul's counsel suggests that Christians should be equally concerned about and respectful of the religious liberty of others—even and perhaps especially that of those who disagree with them.

In planning for the eternal security of heaven and the new earth,[8] God has no place for the use of force to lead a person to accept His will. Those who ultimately enjoy the freedom of heaven will have freely chosen the will of God here.

Many have been puzzled as to how God can give man freedom of choice yet at the same time restrict him through His law. But this should not be difficult to understand. A mother likes to see her children grow and mature. However, before the children are mature, she must guide them with her knowledge, experience, and wisdom. When a little boy wants to play with fire, his mother, in love for her son, either cautions him or prohibits him from getting involved in the danger. God does the same with us, His children.

"But before faith came, we were kept under the law, shut up unto the faith which should afterwards be revealed. Wherefore the law was our schoolmaster to bring us unto Christ, that we might be justified by faith. But after that faith is come, we are no longer under a schoolmaster."[9]

"Till we all come in the unity of the faith, and of the knowledge of the Son of God, unto a perfect man, unto the measure of the stature of the fulness of Christ: that we henceforth be no more children, tossed to and fro, and carried about with every wind of doctrine, by the sleight of men, and cunning craftiness, whereby they lie in wait to deceive; but speaking the truth in love, may grow up into him in all things, which is the head, even Christ."[10]

On a hot day, Esau came back from the field, weary from the hunt and wishing for food and refreshment. He made a completely legitimate request for food, but in his impatience he determined to be gratified even at the cost of his birthright. For a dish of red pottage, he sold his rights as the eldest son of the family. This story illustrates how freedom is often limited. Demanding unlimited freedom may lead one to much difficulty. That is why the apostle Paul admonishes us not to seek our own—it may be neither expedient nor edifying. "All things are lawful for me, but all things are not expedient: all things are lawful for me, but all things edify not. Let no man seek his own, but every man another's wealth."[11]

Modern man is also impatient. He is spoiled by all the modern conveniences around him. He wants instant light, instant heat, instant coolness, and just about everything instantly. He prefers quick-acting pills for assuaging his headache and instant foods for satisfying his hunger. But nature does not always work instantly. Time is needed for one to learn, grow, and mature.

It takes only a year or two for a dog or a cow to grow to physical maturity, but it takes man eighteen years or more. Emotional maturity takes even longer, and character maturity takes a lifetime. We must accept the fact that in possessing freedom of choice, we do not have complete freedom. Total freedom comes when we have complete control of ourselves, and this comes only with full maturity.

As a mother, Ellen G. White once said: "I am a mother; I know whereof I speak, when I say that youth and children are not only safer but happier under wholesome restraint than when following their own inclination. . . . The unbounded freedom granted to children at this age has proved the ruin of thousands."[12]

On the other hand, "God might have created man without the power to transgress His law; He might have withheld the hand of Adam from touching the forbidden fruit; but in that case man would have been, not a free moral agent, but a mere automaton."[13]

Following ancient Chinese emperors around the clock were the recorders who wrote down every word the emperors said. Because what the emperors said became law, this practice of recording helped these rulers to be careful in what they said. We too are judged by our own words. Not long ago a leader of a great nation was judged by his own words on tape. How careful we should be in exercising our freedom!

Throughout the history of Israel, national calamity was used to teach the people the results of failure to live out the law of God. They resorted, therefore, to one device after another to compel themselves to remember the law and to be strict in its observance. They went so far as to attach portions of the law to their bodies or to their doorposts. But they failed to see that God's law written on the heart affects the outward acts. They even made their strictness a wall that insulated them from their heathen neighbors and prevented a faithful witness.

While on earth Jesus did everything according to His Father's will, yet He enjoyed the greatest freedom because sin had no power over Him. He loved God so much that He was perfectly happy to do His will. Wholeheartedly He chose to obey God. God's will became His own. When He carried out God's will, He did it by His own choice. And He says to us, "Take my yoke upon you, and learn of me."[14]

"He [Christ] is a perfect and holy example, given for us to imitate. We cannot equal the pattern; but we shall not be approved of God if we do not copy it and, according to the ability which God has given, resemble it."[15]

To urge us to pattern ourselves after Christ, the apostle Paul admonishes, "Be ye followers of me, even as I also am of Christ."[16] "Those things, which ye have both learned, and received, and heard, and seen in me, do: and the God of peace shall be with you."[17]

It may seem almost presumptuous for Paul to urge his fellow believers to be followers of himself, when he was also human. But he only asked them to follow him to the degree that he was himself a follower of Christ. In the absolute sense, even Paul was not a perfect reproduction of the character of Jesus. But perhaps no other one made more earnest effort to imitate and resemble the divine Pattern. The call is for us to do likewise.

In the call of the gospel are paradoxes—apparently opposing ideas—that a non-Christian may read as contradictions. One pairing of opposing concepts is suggested in the offer of freedom and the call to service (virtually a call to be God's bond servant or slave). Youth especially covet freedom—freedom to think, to explore, to improve on the past. But they—and we—must understand that the truest freedom is to be found in voluntary bondage to the love of Christ.

The love of Christ, in turn, is expressed in the words of the Ten Commandments to meet our situation and condition. He who seeks to do all to the glory of God rather than to his own glory will hold back nothing from the testing of God's holy law. Entire and constant consecration is a small price to pay for eternal joy with God. Such consecration provides perpetual joy now and true freedom forever.

When called by Christ, Paul was not a slave; neither was he a prisoner. When He accepted the commission from Jesus as the apostle to the Gentiles, he gladly called himself a "prisoner of Christ Jesus for the Gentiles."[18] This willingness to submit one's own plans to God is the secret of achieving the highest freedom.

The apostle John, as prisoner on the Isle of Patmos, was also a free man. In the truest sense, he was not a prisoner confined to this earth; he certainly was not a prisoner of sin. But he was free to meet Christ, whose hair appeared "as white as snow," whose "eyes were as a flame of fire," and whose feet were "like unto fine brass, as if they burned in a furnace."[19] John had the freedom of meeting his beloved Master. True freedom is not freedom to sin, but freedom to do God's will.

1. Ellen G. White, *Testimonies*, vol. 5, pp. 173, 174.
2. Luke 18:18-27.
3. Ellen G. White, *Christ's Object Lessons*, p. 392.
4. Ellen G. White, *Selected Messages*, bk. 1, pp. 107, 108.
5. 1 Corinthians 10:27-29.
6. 1 Corinthians 8:9-11.
7. Ellen G. White, *Testimonies*, vol. 9, p. 257.
8. See Nahum 1:9.
9. Galatians 3:23-25.
10. Ephesians 4:13-15.
11. 1 Corinthians 10:23, 24.
12. Ellen G. White, *Fundamentals of Christian Education*, pp. 62, 63.
13. Ellen G. White, *Patriarchs and Prophets*, p. 49.
14. Matthew 11:29.
15. Ellen G. White, *Testimonies*, vol. 2, p. 549.
16. 1 Corinthians 11:1.
17. Philippians 4:9.
18. Ephesians 3:1.
19. Revelation 1:14, 15, NIV.

Respect for Authority

Before Jehovah's awful throne,
Ye nations, bow with sacred joy;
Know that the Lord is God alone;
He can create, and He destroy.[1]

The God we worship is great and powerful. His majesty and great creative power elicit feelings of awe among His worshipers. It appears ironic that we should approach Jehovah's awe-full throne with sacred joy. But through Jesus Christ this is possible.

In many Chinese temples one may find a plaque with these words on it: "Respect God as though God were here." Even though we cannot see God with our physical eyes, when we go to church to worship Him, we should discern Him with our spiritual eyes and respect Him. He is there in the church to receive our praise and adoration. By virtue of His power and authority, He alone deserves our worship and praise.

The traditional concepts of authority are reflected in the accepted definitions of it. Authority, according to Webster, is the "Power to influence or command thought, opinion, or behavior." Authority also means "freedom granted by one in authority."[2]

A father has authority over his children because he participates in giving them life, in nurturing them to adulthood, and in educating them.

An employer has authority over his subordinates because he pays them wages based on a certain formula and has entered into a contract for their services, including the use of their time, energy, and talents.

In days gone by, a king had authority over his subjects because it was believed that the king was ordained of God to rule. In China the emperor was called "tientze"—the "Son of Heaven." Since God created everything and owns everything, He has the supreme authority. But God may delegate some of His authority to a king to exercise.

These are traditional concepts of authority, and some are still valid today. However, because of rapidly increasing knowledge and an emphasis on the relationship of the individual citizen to the whole of society, the idea of democracy has gradually gained widespread support. The democratic principle is reflected not only in political systems but also in decision-making processes, in concepts of social-welfare services, and even in tax structures.

In a democracy, when the authority of the chief executive is delegated to him by the voters his authority arises. We ultimately trace the origin of their authority back to God. All power and authority must come from the Life-giver, the Creator.

The apostle Paul admonishes us to respect the authority of the government. Governments may be ineffective, corrupt, and even oppressive. But when a government enacts a law—good or bad—the right thing to do is to respect and obey it, unless of course, it conflicts with God's law. "Let every soul be subject unto the higher powers. For there is no power but of God: the powers that be are ordained of God. Whosoever therefore resisteth the power, resisteth the ordinance of God: and they that resist shall receive to themselves damnation."[3]

In the experience of Israel, "God was the center of authority and government. Moses, as His representative, was to administer the laws in His name. Then came the council of seventy, then the priests and the princes, under these 'captains over fifties, and captains over tens' (Numbers 11:16, 17; Deuteronomy 1:15), and lastly, officers appointed for special duties."[4]

In our present-day experiences, we often see the power of "captains," "princes," and "officers," but seldom do we think of them as servants of God from whom they have received authority.

Even in church elections the officers elected by the congregation receive their authority from God, "the center of authority and government." Like the apostles, they administer the church business in God's name.

On government envelopes in Commonwealth countries are the words, "On Her Majesty's Service." We also are servants of God, doing His business.

The authority of the church does not reside in itself but in the Lord, who founded it and called it to administer His authority in His absence. He has not left it without a charter. He has placed supreme authority in His Word as interpreted to us by the Spirit of truth. In this Word are recorded the unchanging, eternal principles which express God's own character.[5]

Jesus Christ, the Founder of both the Old and New Testament churches, provides by His atonement the only basis by which His law may be written in the hearts of believing sinners. Thus the atonement undergirds the authority of the church.

God's servants are ordained by Him to do His work on earth. Even though they are human and make mistakes, they are still His chosen representatives.

"Those who despise and reject the faithful servant of God show contempt, not merely for the man, but for the Master who sent him. It is God's words, His reproofs and counsel, that are set at nought; it is His authority that is rejected."[6]

About paying taxes to the government, the apostle Paul says: "For this cause pay ye tribute also: for they are God's ministers, attending continually upon this very thing."[7]

In the days of the Roman Empire the government was headed by a caesar, some of whom were good and some bad. When Paul wrote the epistle of Romans, Nero, a wicked king, was on the throne in Rome. Nevertheless, Paul admonished the Roman Christians that they should not evade tax but be honest in paying it. Should we not also respect the government even if we do not approve of its policies?

Unfortunately, some ambitious and selfish people take God's authority into their hands and use it to exploit others to their own advantage. The abuse of authority is very common, both in history and in our world today. The corruption, exploitation, and cruelty of some authorities has exhausted the patience of frustrated citizens, leading to demonstrations, strikes and revolutions. The trial and sentencing of the so-called Gang of Four and their followers in China could not fully answer to the magnitude of the injustice done. The punishment of a few is hardly sufficient to quench the anger of the victims or their friends and relatives. It is easy to see how respect for authority has eroded.

In the twentieth century, wars and revolutions have changed many governments—not only in form, but in ideology. These clashing ideologies create increasing tension and conflict among the authorities. Authority is widely under attack in today's world, and respect for authority sinks to low levels. And when there is no respect for authority, anarchy rules.

"In the kingdoms of the world, position meant self-aggrandizement. The people were supposed to exist for the benefit of the ruling classes. Influence, wealth, education, were so many means of gaining control of the masses for the use of the leaders. The higher classes were to think, decide, enjoy, and rule; the lower were to obey and serve. Religion, like all things else, was a matter of authority. The people were expected to believe and practice as their superiors directed. The right of man as man, to think and act for himself, was wholly unrecognized."[8]

In a home, the father is the king and the mother is the queen. They are responsible for making the home a little Eden for themselves and their children. The father, who is also the priest, should take the family to God's altar every day that they may all know Him.

"Parents, make home happy for your children. . . . If you allow them to do as they please, their purity and loveliness of character will quickly fade. Teach them to obey. Let them see that your authority must be respected."[9]

There are times when the authority of the government is in conflict with that of God. Since God's authority is supreme and His law infallible, we must place our first loyalty on God's side. The climax of the great controversy will be Satan's attempt to force God's people to disobey Him. This he will do with the help of legislators.

"We are to recognize human government as an ordinance of divine appointment, and teach obedience to it as a sacred duty, within its legitimate sphere. But when its claims conflict with the claims of God, we must obey God rather than men. God's word must be recognized as above all human legislation. A 'Thus saith the Lord' is not to be set aside for a 'Thus saith the church' or a 'Thus saith the state.' The crown of Christ is to be lifted above the diadems of earthly potentates."[10]

"The authorities will make laws to restrict religious liberty. They will assume the right that is God's alone. They will think they can force the conscience, which God alone should control. Even now they are making a beginning; this work they will continue to carry forward till they reach a boundary over which they cannot step. God will interpose in behalf of His loyal, commandment-keeping people."[11]

In different parts of the world at present we see a revival of the call for government enforcement of moral principles, regardless of individual convictions.

"The Bible plainly teaches that a time is approaching when the laws of the state will so conflict with the law of God that whosoever would obey all the divine precepts must brave reproach and punishment as an evildoer."[12]

A Chinese proverb says, "If one has not done guilty things during the day, he has nothing to fear when someone knocks on his door at midnight." Only criminals are afraid of the police. "For rulers are not a terror to good works, but to the evil. Wilt thou then not be afraid of the power? do that which is good, and thou shalt have praise of the same."[13]

If fear were not at work, no amount of law enforcement would suffice to maintain law and order. With some citizens a sense of honor and self-respect steers them away from doing wrong. But with others only the fear of being caught and punished deters them from violating the law.

While not a positive motive, fear nonetheless serves a purpose in a society full of wickedness. Fear can deter. But unfortunately it has little power to reform. Only love can cause a sinner to repent.

If God had destroyed Satan when he first rebelled, or if Adam and Eve had died immediately after partaking of the forbidden fruit, all creatures in the universe would have been so afraid of God that they would never again have believed that God is love. In His great mercy God allowed sin to develop and reveal its effects. He also allowed the plan of salvation to unfold in order to demonstrate His eternal love for men.

Fear has definite limitations in its power to reform. For example, smoking is hazardous to one's health. But because smoking does not immediately bring death, people continue to smoke. Only those with wisdom know what to choose and what not to choose. To fear and refrain from doing it are signs of maturity. Only little children need constant supervision.

Yet many worship their gods because they are afraid. They respect these gods because of the authority they have over people. Their guilty consciences tell them that their gods will punish them if they do not respect the gods or plead for mercy before them. If they do enough to please their gods, these gods may condescend to bestow blessings upon them.

But the Christian God is a different God. Yes, He is great. He is powerful. He is like fire. He cannot tolerate sin. But He is also a merciful God, a God of love, a God of forgiveness. At His throne love and justice meet. His character is a combination of mercy and justice. We should respect Him; we should have a feeling of awe before Him. But this awe-full feeling should not prevent us from coming to Him just as we are.

The reason we don't have to be afraid of Him is because Jesus Christ, our High Priest, has paid the penalty for our sins and has given us His robe of righteousness that we may not be shown filthy or naked before God. "Let us therefore come boldly unto the throne of grace, that we may obtain mercy, and find grace to help in time of need."[14]

Some may indeed do good because of fear. But in this sinful world another major motive for doing good is love.

There are many sources of power in the world today—brute force, the power of armaments, the power of wealth, the power of superior education, the power of intellect, the power of persuasion, and the power of the majority. But any and all of these may tend to corruption on the part of those who exercise such power and to rebellion on the part of those dominated by it. Love is different. It seeks only the benefit of its recipient. Like the Heavenly Merchantman, it only stands at the door and knocks. It does not batter the door down!

When every other means of persuasion has failed, love may find a way.[15] It is both quiet and all-persuasive in its operation.

For complex reasons, many people today seem reluctant to be law-abiding citizens. They try to find ways to evade or circumvent the law, often obeying it only because they fear its penalty.

Every parent and every teacher is troubled at some time over the question of disciplining children. The long reign of a permissive philosophy has increased the size of the discipline problem. Firm gentleness or gentle firmess is called for.

"Wherever the power of intellect, of authority, or of force is employed, and love is not manifestly present, the affections and will of those whom we seek to reach assume a defensive, repelling position, and their strength of resistance is increased. Jesus was the Prince of Peace. He came into the world to bring resistance and authority into subjection to Himself. Wisdom and strength He could command, but the means He employed with which to overcome evil were the wisdom and strength of love."[16]

The Christian should undoubtedly be the most outstanding example of law-abiding citizenry in his community. When the Christian's life is motivated by the law-loving example and justifying righteousness of Jesus Christ, his will is continually given up to the will of the Lord. He does not follow his own inclinations or depend upon himself for the carrying out of the will of Heaven. "Obedience is the Highest dictate of reason as well as of conscience."[17]

As servants of Christ we are all involved in obeying our Master. "Obedience to God is of more value to you than gold or silver. Yoking up with Christ, learning His meekness and lowliness, cuts short many a conflict; for when the enemy comes in like a flood, the Spirit of the Lord lifts up a standard against him."[18]

"It is better to request than to command; the one thus addressed has opportunity to prove himself loyal to right principles. His obedience is the result of choice rather than compulsion."[19]

For God's law is of a different kind. It is a moral law governing even our motives, but it is unenforceable by human beings. Our conscience, enlightened by the Word and the Spirit, is God's agent for enforcing His law. God loves us and wants us to return that love by willingly obeying His law. And if we accept His law as our inward law, we will have no problem in choosing to obey Him.

1. *Church Hymnal,* no. 1.
2. *Webster's New Collegiate Dictionary.*
3. Romans 13:1, 2.
4. Ellen G. White, *Education,* p. 37.
5. See Hebrews 13:8.
6. Ellen G. White, *Patriarchs and Prophets,* p. 605.
7. Romans 13:6.

8. Ellen G. White, *The Desire of Ages*, p. 550.
9. Ellen G. White, *Child Guidance*, p. 271.
10. Ellen G. White, *The Acts of the Apostles*, p. 69.
11. Ellen G. White, *The Desire of Ages*, p. 630.
12. Ellen G. White, *The Great Controversy*, p. 459.
13. Romans 13:3.
14. Hebrews 4:16.
15. See 1 Corinthians 13.
16. Ellen G. White, *Testimonies*, vol. 2, pp. 135, 136.
17. Ellen G. White, *The Acts of the Apostles*, p. 506.
18. Ellen G. White, *Testimonies*, vol. 8, p. 95.
19. Ellen G. White, *Education*, p. 290.

Sabbath—A Foretaste
of Heaven

After creating the earth and everything in it, God set up an institution—the Sabbath—to be a channel through which He might bless mankind. Even in the Garden of Eden where there was no sin, God saw the need for setting aside one seventh of time for man to communicate with Him; for He knows our need to fellowship with Him. "Man shall not live by bread alone, but by every word that proceedeth out of the mouth of God."[1]

By studying God's Word and thus fellowshiping with Him, we grow not only intellectually but spiritually. Peace, harmony, and joy—the atmosphere of heaven—continue as long as we remain closely united to God through His Word and through fellowshiping with Him each Sabbath.

With the loss of Paradise, man's original peace was forfeited. Adam and Eve could no longer have face-to-face fellowship with God as they did in the Garden of Eden. But God has promised that He will continue to bless us as we keep our appointment with Him each Sabbath. He will continue to fellowship with us and bless us with a foretaste of heaven—the peace enjoyed by Adam and Eve in the Garden of Eden.

In order to accept this gift of heavenly peace, mankind must believe in God. Ancient Israel died in the wilderness and lost the rest they could have enjoyed in Canaan because they did not possess a faith that led to obedience. "They despised my judgments, and walked not in my statutes, but polluted my sabbaths: for their heart went after their idols."[2]

Fellowship with God on the Sabbath—rightly observed—reminds us of the cross and the resurrection and draws us to holiness and obedience. We are busy with our own affairs for six days of the week. But on the Sabbath—the seventh day—God wants us to pause and contemplate His creation and redemption, renewing our friendship with Him and reviewing our relation to our fellowmen. When we cease to meet with God, we become selfish tyrants in our own "kingdom." We become proud and self-centered. Our love toward God and our fellowmen diminishes. To help counteract these tendencies, God has designed that we should keep the Sabbath. By keeping the Sabbath, we are reminded that we are created by God, our loving heavenly Father. We learn to know those who call the same God their Father as our brothers and sisters.

On the Sabbath, by coming into communion with God, we enter a holy atmosphere akin to the peace that Adam and Eve enjoyed in the Garden of Eden. By having faith in God, we may gain what ancient Israel lost. In this atmosphere of fellowship with God and meditation upon Jesus, we will become like Him. That wall which separates us from God will be removed.

Being united with God by faith, we shall be sanctified—be wholly consecrated—"without which [holiness] no man shall see the Lord."[3] The presence of God sanctifies. By entering into His holy presence in holy time—the Sabbath—our sanctification deepens. "I gave them my sabbaths, to be a sign between me and them, that they might know that I am the Lord that sanctify them."[4]

The Sabbath has been given to the world as the sign that God is both the Creator and Sanctifier. The power that created all material and living things is the power that re-creates the soul in God's own likeness. The Sabbath day is a sign of sanctification to those who keep it holy. True sanctification is harmony with God. It is manifest in loving obedience to the law—those principles that are the transcript of God's character. The Sabbath becomes the sign of obedience to the one who, from the heart, obeys the fourth commandment. "Obedience to all the commandments of God is the only true sign of sanctification."[5]

"We are to bear witness to all nations, kindreds, and tongues that we are a people who love and fear God, a people who keep holy His memorial of creation, the sign between Him and His obedient children that He sanctifies them."[6]

"The Sabbath is a sign of Christ's power to make us holy. And it is given to all whom Christ makes holy. As a sign of His sanctifying power, the Sabbath is given to all who through Christ become a part of the Israel of God."[7]

"According to the fourth commandment the Sabbath was dedicated to rest and religious worship. All secular employment was to be suspended, but works of mercy and benevolence were in accordance with the purpose of the Lord. They were not to be limited to time or place. To relieve the afflicted, to comfort the sorrowing, is a labor of love that does honor to God's holy day."[8] "The work of Christ in healing the sick was in perfect accord with the law. It honored the Sabbath."[9]

The Lord of the Sabbath is certainly a safe example for us to follow in our observance of the day. For Him it was not a day of idleness or merely a catch-up-on-sleep day following the labor and activity of the week. It was a day of worship in synagogue and on mountain—a day of fellowship with those dear to Him and those to whom He ministered. It was a day of showing mercy and bringing healing to the needy souls everywhere present. Not by His design was it a day of controversy; but it became such, at times, as the Lord sought to defend His day against the erroneous attitudes toward it which had grown up over the centuries of Israel's checkered experience.

The Jewish teachers failed to see in the Sabbath God's sweet invitation to keep an appointment with Him—a personal and loving God, the Creator and Sustainer of life and all things in the universe.

As Sabbath keepers, we may at times place too much emphasis on what we should *not* do rather that what we *should* do. Seeing the Sabbath from a negative viewpoint, we make Sabbath keeping something passive, joyless, and even grudging. In order to enjoy the kind of Sabbath rest which Adam and Eve enjoyed in the Garden of Eden, we must have faith and be willing to accept God's restoration in our hearts of the rest and eventually the eternal peace that we will enjoy in the new earth.

Therefore the Sabbath is a foretaste of heaven. In addition to being a memorial of Creation, the Sabbath also points us to the rest and happiness we will enjoy in the future when God comes to abolish sin and re-create a beautiful world for all who desire to meet Him each Sabbath through eternity. Unless we really want to meet God on the Sabbath, we will not develop a desire to meet Him when He comes.

The fourth commandment is stated positively. It is a command to be and to do something. Unlike the commandments couched in the setting of "thou shalt not," this commandment exhorts us to remember and to keep the Sabbath.

As with the rest of the Ten Commandments, the fourth deals with spirit as well as letter. With the best of intentions, the Jewish teachers hedged in the Sabbath with multiple regulations of their own invention in an effort to enforce upon the people the sacred observance of the day. They knew that their checkered history was in part the result of forgetting the Sabbath. But there is no blessing in keeping the letter of the law. Sabbath, to be a joy and blessing, must be a special time devoted to fellowship with our best Friend. But if we have no relationship with Him, the Sabbath is a burden and a bore—a good work grudgingly performed with the hope of avoiding a penalty.

To reject out of hand the "mechanics" of Sabbath observance is not wise. As kneeling reinforces the spirit of reverence, so acts of Sabbath respect may strengthen our sense of its sacredness. Even so, the externals of Sabbath keeping may be stressed too much.

"The rabbis reduced the Sabbath to an absurdity by their rigid and meaningless distinction between what might and what might not be done on that day. They emphasized the negative aspect of Sabbath observance of refraining from certain things. The forms of religion were set forth as the substance of it."[10]

God meant it when He said that the Sabbath was made for man. Man was created before the Sabbath was made. God needed no rest from His labors. But man needed a continual reminder that God is the Creator and Sustainer of all. He also needed a special time in which to put aside the joyous labors of Eden and devote himself wholly to fellowship with and worship of His God. The Sabbath therefore was made for man. The fact that man soon forgot what God had told him is evidence enough of how much he needed the command to "remember."

"God did not create man because He had a Sabbath and needed someone to keep it. Rather, an all-wise Creator knew that man, the creature of His hand, needed opportunity for moral and spiritual growth, for character development. He needed time in which his own interest and pursuits should be subordinated to a study of the character and will of God as revealed in nature, and later, in revelation. The seventh-day Sabbath was ordained of God to meet this need. To tamper in any way with the Creator's specifications as to when and how the day should be observed is tantamount to denying that God knows what is best for the creatures of His hand.

"God ordained that the Sabbath should be a blessing, not a burden, and it is to man's interest and not his injury to observe it. It was designed to increase his happiness, not to work a hardship on him."[11]

Just as Adam and Eve were invited to enjoy the beauty of creation and fellowship with God on their first Sabbath, the invitation for fellowship is extended to each Christian. God desires to come down to converse with His children. For them this should be a very joyous experience. Like children who enjoy seeing their father returning home from work, the children of God should be eagerly waiting for the arrival of the Sabbath as the time in which they have happy fellowship with their God.

Since Eden was lost and we are no longer able to see God face-to-face, the Sabbath should be a special day—a moment of delight in God's presence. When we feel His presence, our minds are lifted above the worldly and unimportant. We experience a freedom from the toil and problems of life and enjoy a peace which only God can bestow.

In this atmosphere of fellowship with God, we find peace with God, ourselves, and our fellowmen. Sin loses its dominion over us. Through the Holy Spirit, we enjoy communion with Jesus, who is Emmanuel, "God with us."[12]

In communing with God, we study His words, pray, and partake of the bread and wine, which symbolize His body and His blood. The Sabbath provides us time to meet God and commune with Him in these various ways.

In order fully to enjoy the Sabbath, we must have faith to invite God into our hearts and be willing to accept the fourth commandment as a covenant. Unfortunately, the ancient Israelites, because of unbelief, were not allowed to enter the land of rest. Therefore God promised that "there remains a sabbath rest for the people of God."[13]

In this world, men are stratified into classes: the very rich, the rich, the middle class, and the poor. In the hierarchies of the military, the government, and commercial or industrial organizations, superiors are separated from subordinates by virtue of their positions. These might have been good friends before such a separation, but now their positions may dictate that they deal with each other according to their new roles and expectations.

In medieval times the lives of the poor were not

considered as being of much value. Even today the poor are being exploited. The handicapped, disadvantaged, uneducated, and aged are all often looked down upon as well.

But the Sabbath restores in us all the human dignity we should enjoy. On the Sabbath especially, being in the presence of God makes even the most lowly a prince. We can forget our toil, our want, and our suffering. We are liberated from these because in Christ all are equal—all are God's children. Jesus Christ places a high value on every soul, even on the smallest and youngest one. He was willing to die for the most lowly, the most wicked, the most unintelligent.

On Sabbath all other things become unimportant, and God becomes all-important. On this day He becomes our honored Guest, our Teacher, our Physician, our Saviour, and our King. At the same time, we become His children, His patients, His students, and by His invitation, His guests.

In this beautiful relationship, we become new creatures. We are sanctified. We do not need to force ourselves to obey Him. We love to learn to do His will. Let us enter into this new relationship with God by keeping the Sabbath and enjoying all the goodness He is waiting to bestow on us. In this way, the Sabbath can truly be a blessing to us.

1. Matthew 4:4.
2. Ezekiel 20:16.
3. Hebrews 12:14.
4. Ezekiel 20:12.
5. Ellen G. White Comments, *S.D.A. Bible Commentary*, vol. 7, p. 908.
6. Ellen G. White, *Testimonies*, vol. 7, p. 107.
7. Ellen G. White, *The Desire of Ages*, p. 288.
8. Ellen G. White, *Welfare Ministry*, p. 77.
9. Ellen G. White, *The Desire of Ages*, p. 207.
10. *S.D.A. Bible Commentary*, vol. 5, p. 589.
11. *S.D.A. Bible Commentary*, vol. 5, p. 588.
12. Matthew 1:22
13. Hebrews 4:9, RSV.

The Beginning of Human Relations

In a society, the importance of human relations is taken for granted. Of all the different kinds of human relations governed by the inward law, one of the most basic is that between a child and his parents. Out of this relationship a child learns to relate—either poorly or well—to all other people. If he does not have a satisfying relationship with his parents, both the development of his personality and his other human relationships may be jeopardized. Fathers, mothers, and children have roles in the family that exist nowhere else.

For children to love parents is usually quite natural. Love for parents may be expressed in speaking words of affection to them or in doing something for them. Children who thus show love and respect for their parents, the Bible says, will receive a blessing from heaven and will live long on the earth.

"Parents are entitled to a degree of love and respect which is due to no other person. God Himself, who has placed upon them a responsibility for the soul committed to their charge, has ordained that during the earlier years of life, parents shall stand in the place of God to their children. And he who rejects the rightful authority of his parents is rejecting the authority of God. The fifth commandment requires children not only to yield respect, submission, and obedience to their parents, but also to give them love and tenderness, to lighten their cares, to guard their reputation, and to succor and comfort them in old age."[1]

"Not only is it natural that obedience should be given to parents, but it is God's express will. It is the first commandment in the Decalogue to which a promise is specifically attached; indeed, it is altogether unique in that respect. . . . Special blessing is promised upon those who obey their parents."[2]

The apostle Paul admonishes Christian young people, "Children, obey your parents in the Lord: for this is right."[3] However, since parents are human, and since some of them might not have accepted Christ, children are told to obey them "in the Lord." If the parents' wishes or commands are contrary to the Lord's, children should obey the Lord, for He has higher wisdom, and His way is perfect.

Children also should respect their parents—especially when the parents are elderly, sick, or handicapped. At such times and under such circumstances, parents most need the sympathy, love, and support of their children. Even though parents may have adequate wealth and be physically well cared for, they have psychological and emotional needs. Their loneliness and their hunger for love can be satisfied by receiving genuine love from their children.

Sons and daughters should seek no excuse for failing to show love to their parents. Jesus once condemned the Pharisees for their cold, legalistic attitudes toward their parents. While no law can compel sons or daughters to love their parents, children should rely on no tradition or custom as an excuse for not fulfilling this inward-law commandment of love.

For thousands of years the Chinese have emphasized this important aspect of human relations. They realize that unless parents and children form strong bonds of love, there can be no good relations among brothers and sisters, friends and associates, teachers and students, or kings and subjects.

Could this strong family emphasis perhaps have contributed to the long history of the Chinese, in fulfillment of the promise in the fifth commandment?[4] While many other major ancient civilizations have vanished and some of their great peoples have scattered, the Chinese people have maintained their own integrity and culture through the ages. This even though they have been repeatedly invaded by barbarians, who were then later absorbed into the total culture and people.

To be considered in connection with the fifth commandment is the principle that parents are to teach and love their children in such a way that the children will return continuing respect and honor to their parents. Children deserve the attention and love of their parents, without which they may grow up not knowing how to accept or respond to love. Into the vacuum created by a lack of love may rush suspicion, alienation, and even hatred, in the hearts of such children. And when they grow up, they often bring heartaches to their parents and problems to society.

"When children love and repose confidence in their mother, and have become obedient to her, they have been taught the first lessons in becoming Christians."[5]

Today more and more young mothers are working outside the home—many times out of economic necessity. This makes God's ideal for the home much more difficult to attain. How can the mother be the child's sunshine in the most protective and comforting place on earth if she cannot be there much of the time? So often she must entrust to another—who does not always have reason to care as she does—the privilege of loving and training her child.

And what about fathers? God's messenger has this counsel for them: "Fathers, spend as much time as possible with your children. Seek to become acquainted with their various dispositions, that you may know how to train them in harmony with the word of God. Never should a word of discouragement pass your lips. Do not bring darkness into the home. Be pleasant, kind, and affectionate toward your children, but not foolishly indulgent. Let them bear their little disappointments, as every one must. Do not encourage them to come to you with their petty complaints of one another. Teach them to bear with one another and to seek to maintain each other's confidence and respect."[6]

While it is possible for parents to become dictatorial, it is also possible for parents to abdicate their role as authority figures. In a home there are matters for which parents must be responsible and which demand decisions. Parents should discipline themselves so that they may in turn discipline their children.

Each child is different from another—even from a twin. Therefore each should be considered individually, yet not treated partially or preferentially. The expression of love may also need to differ, so that one child will not feel starved while another is overindulged. Moreover, siblings must know that they are equally important and equally loved. Here the difficulty parents face is in deciding how best to bestow love to each child.

Unless children are taught to honor their parents, not only in words, but by example, they will not know how to do so.

"Teach your children to honor you, because the law of God lays this duty upon children. If you allow your children to lightly esteem your wishes and pay no regard to the laws of the household, you are winking at sin; you are permitting the devil to work as he will; and the same insubordination, want of reverence, and love of self will be carried with them even into the religious life and into the church."[7]

Our children, after all, know best what kind of Christians we are. They sense almost instinctively when all is well. They are quick to forgive, whenever we are able to bring ourselves to acknowledge our failing and wrongs to them. They can even forgive us for the contrast that all too often exists between our church-pew image and our home fireside image.

In an industrialized urban environment where seemingly everyone works or studies, the care of the elderly at home may pose quite a dilemma. Once this topic was hotly debated between a Westernized Chinese and a traditional Chinese. The former felt that it is a crime to keep the aging parent home where he cannot get adequate physical care. But the latter contended that it is more cruel to send the aging parent to an impersonal institution and let him die in loneliness.

The question is how much time or how much money are the children willing and able to give? If a daughter is willing to quit her job and stay home to take care of an elderly parent, she provides the comfort and love that would be difficult to find in an institution. On the other hand, if everyone in the family must work, a nursing home may be far better than leaving a parent without adequate care.

Since the situation in each family is different, there can be no one best rule. Mutual understanding and agreement between parent and child as to the best arrangement is the key to satisfaction. We need constantly to consider our motives in what we do for those who are too young or too old to defend themselves against our handling of their affairs.

Jesus is our model. The Bible records that "he went down with them [His parents], and came to Nazareth, and was subject to them."[8] "Jesus lived in a peasant's home, and faithfully and cheerfully acted His part in bearing the burdens of the household. He had been the Commander of heaven, and angels had delighted to fulfill His word; now He was a willing servant, a loving, obedient son. He learned a trade, and with His own hands worked in the carpenter's shop with Joseph."[9]

"Jesus did not ignore His relation to His earthy parents. From Jerusalem He returned home with them, and aided them in their life of toil. . . For eighteen years after He had recognized that He was the Son of God, He acknowledged the tie that bound Him to the home at Nazareth, and performed the duties of a son, a brother, a friend, and a citizen."[10]

Even when nailed on the cross, Jesus did not forget His mother or her needs. "Looking into her grief-stricken face and then upon John, He said to her, 'Woman, behold thy son!' then to John, 'Behold thy mother!' John understood Christ's words. and accepted the trust. He at once took Mary to his home, and from that hour cared for her tenderly. O pitiful, loving

Saviour; amid all His physical pain and mental anguish, He had a thoughtful care for His mother! He had no money with which to provide for her comfort; but He was enshrined in the heart of John, and He gave His mother to him as a precious legacy. Thus He provided for her that which she most needed,—the tender sympathy of one who loved her because she loved Jesus. . . .

"The perfect example of Christ's filial love shines forth with undimmed luster from the mist of ages. . . . Even in His last agony, He remembers to provide for His sorrowing, widowed mother. The same spirit will be seen in every disciple of our Lord. Those who follow Christ will feel that it is a part of their religion to respect and provide for their parents."[11]

Those who have grown up reciting the Lord's Prayer may have little insight into the nature of the title Jesus gave to the Sovereign of the universe when He introduced Him as "Our Father." The Hebrew concept of God stressed His power, majesty, rulership, and awesomeness. It gave little stress to the paternal warmth of divine love and care.

Most of us who have been blessed in our childhood and youth with a loving and lovable human father can little understand the problems faced by those who have not. For such, the suggestion that God is a "Father" can often convey negative impressions. Soul winners need to keep this possibility in mind as they witness and to offer their hearers other names and symbols of God that will have more positive connotations in their experience.

In calling God our Father, we recognize our fellowmen as brothers and sisters. We extend our family circle to include all who call Him "heavenly Father." When this new relation is fully recognized and established in the new earth, there will be no war, crime, or hatred. Only love will rule in the hearts of men.

"For as the heaven is high above the earth, so great is his mercy toward them that fear him. As far as the east is from the west, so far hath he removed our transgressions from us. Like as a father pitieth his children, so the Lord pitieth them that fear him."[12]

1. Ellen G. White, *Patriarchs and Prophets*, p. 308.
2. *S.D.A. Bible Commentary*, vol. 6, p. 1040.
3. Ephesians 6:1.
4. Ephesians 6:2, 3.
5. Ellen G. White, *My Life Today*, p. 164.
6. Ellen G. White, *The Adventist Home*, p. 222.
7. Ellen G. White, *Child Guidance*, pp. 87, 88.
8. Luke 2:51.
9. Ellen G. White, *The Desire of Ages*, p. 72.
10. Ellen G. White, *The Desire of Ages*, p. 82.
11. Ellen G. White, *The Desire of Ages*, p. 752.
12. Psalm 103:11-13.

Life—An Irreplaceable Gift

Life is sacred because God created it and because—other than God—no one can create it. Once life is taken, no human effort can remedy the loss. With life gone, wealth, fame, power, or even love mean nothing. In order to enjoy any of these, man must have life.

We all have life in us, and we observe the life of animals and plants. But what is life? With the aid of modern medical equipment, an unconscious person may be kept alive. Therefore consciousness is not life. We all recognize that there is life even in a sleeping person.

The opposite of life is death—coldness, immobility, silence, and the absence of all vital signs. Death also means decay, decomposition, and, usually, disappearance. While some have had their thoughts written down, their speeches recorded on tape, or their activities recorded on film or videotape, the great majority of the world's people disappear from view at death and after only a few decades are no longer remembered. They just pass into oblivion. We may remember grandpa or grandma, but few of us have had any contact with or carry any memory of great-grandpa or great-grandma.

God is the Creator of life. In Him, and only in Him, is life. When God created man, He "breathed into his nostrils the breath of life; and man became a living soul."[1] From the beginning we all have inherited life. "In Jesus is our life derived. In Him is life, that is original, unborrowed, underived life. In us there is a streamlet from the fountain of life. In Him is the fountain of life."[2]

But God did not just create life and leave all living things to run their own course. Rather, He has continued to give life and breath to each of His creatures. He sustains life every moment. "The God who made the world and everything in it . . . gives to all men life and breath and everything."[3] "God is the life-giver. From the beginning all His laws were ordained to life."[4] "All life-giving power is from Him."[5] "In God we live and move and have our being. Each heart-beat, each breath, is the inspiration of Him who breathed into the nostrils of Adam the breath of life."[6]

If man had continued to live in God's love and had obeyed Him, he would have continued to enjoy the fruit of the tree of life and would have lived forever. Unfortunately, he lost paradise; and death—or the absence of life—has come to mankind. In fact, we lose vitality every moment. Aging is nothing but the process of losing life.

Inasmuch as life is so precious, we must never give any thought to taking life. We should do everything we can to preserve life—that of others and our own. In the fifth chapter of Matthew, Jesus Christ took the opportunity to enlarge the definition of killing.[7] If we hate or become angry with someone, God regards it as if we are taking the person's life—or at least a portion of it. Likewise, if one hates himself or becomes intemperate, he also is regarded by God as taking his own life. Killing—regardless of its form—is a violation of the sixth commandment.

God is love. In love He gave man life. Jesus said, "I am come that they might have life, and that they might have it more abundantly."[8] In order to show us a more complete, meaningful, and fruitful life, He came to earth to live among men. He came to show God's love. He came to show us a life which has no trace of hatred but is full of only love. We who live in the valley of the shadow of death are very prone to fall for the temptation to hate or to be intemperate. Only in God's love can we regain what we have lost and find life abundant.

In the minds of some kings or generals, the lives of peasants or soldiers might be nearly worthless, yet in God's eyes every soul is precious. The value of life can be understood only in light of Calvary. It takes the life of God's Son to redeem the life of a sinner. We are told that for only one sinner, Jesus would have endured Calvary. What matchless love!

"Christ endured shame and agony and death for us. . . . Jesus died, not only to make atonement for us, but to be our pattern. Oh, wondrous condescension! matchless love!"[9]

In order to allow the innocent a chance against the law of revenge, provision was made in ancient Israel to protect the unintentional offenders from revenge by relatives of the victims.[10]

Compared to the laws of other nations and cultures of the day, the laws of Israel showed a profound respect for human life. In a trial for murder the accused was not to be condemned on the testimony of one witness, even though circumstantial evidence might be strong against him. The Lord's direction was, "Whoso killeth any person, the murderer shall be put to death by the mouth of witnesses: but one witness shall not testify against any person to cause him to die."[11]

At the same time, should the guilt of the one accused of murder be substantiated by adequate testimony, the sentencing and punishment must not be avoided. "Whoso sheddeth man's blood, by man shall his blood be shed."[12] "Ye shall take no satisfaction for the life of a murderer, which is guilty of death: but he shall be surely put to death. . . . The land cannot be cleansed of the blood that is shed therein, but by the blood of him that shed it."[13] "Thou shalt take him from mine altar, that he may die."[14]

In Christ we find "a city of refuge" where we can escape vengeful hands. Even this life is precious, for once it is taken, nobody can give it back except God perform a miracle. And God also will not hastily sentence a man to the second death. Instead, He gives him a hearing, allowing Christ to be his attorney-at-law and substitute.

Murder is an awful crime. The Lord has plainly and specifically commanded: "Thou shalt not kill."[15] "All acts of injustice that tend to shorten life; the spirit of hatred and revenge, or the indulgence of any passion that leads to injurious acts toward others, or causes us even to wish them harm (for 'whosoever hateth his brother is a murderer'); a selfish neglect of caring for the needy or suffering; all these are, to a greater or lesser degree, violations of the sixth commandment."[16]

In the system of justice ordained by the God of Israel, there was to be no partiality shown the accused on account of rank or wealth. The Lord even held a city or community accountable if it conspired with the accused to work out an exemption from punishment in the event of murder. "The Lord designed to impress upon His people the terrible guilt of murder, while He would make the most thorough and merciful provision for the acquittal of the innocent."[17]

"Cain the murderer was soon called to answer for his crime. . . . God had given Cain an opportunity to confess his sin. He had had time to reflect. He knew the enormity of the deed he had done, and of the falsehood he had uttered to conceal it; but he was rebellious still, and sentence was no longer deferred. The divine voice that had been heard in entreaty and admonition pronounced the terrible words: 'And now art thou cursed from the earth, which hath opened her mouth to receive thy brother's blood from thy hand. When thou tillest the ground, it shall not henceforth yield unto thee her strength; a fugitive and a vagabond shalt thou be in the earth.' "[18]

The clear teaching of Jesus is that murder exists first in the mind. Hatred in the heart becomes the motive for killing. "Envy is the offspring of pride, and, if it is entertained in the heart, it will lead to cruel deeds, to hatred, revenge, and murder."[19]

"It was envy that made Saul miserable and put the

humble subject of his throne in jeopardy. What untold mischief has this evil trait of character worked in our world! The same enmity existed in the heart of Saul that stirred the heart of Cain against his brother Abel, because Abel's works were righteous, and God honored him, and his own works were evil, and the Lord could not bless him. Envy is the offspring of pride, and if it is entertained in the heart, it will lead to hatred, and eventually to revenge and murder. Satan displayed his own character in exciting the fury of Saul against him who had never done him harm."[20]

Men's consciences are becoming totally benumbed, and murder is becoming extremely common. Governments draft their young people into the armed forces and teach them to kill. In wars atrocious killers receive medals for gallantry from their political leaders. Novels and TV shows portray killing as of little consequence. Should anyone be surprised that murders are sharply on the increase?

A cannibal is supposed to have once asked a civilized person, "Why do you kill so many people in war? You cannot eat them all! Is it not rather wasteful to kill so many?"

Who has the higher ethical standard—the cannibal or the so-called civilized person?

Besides killing fellow human beings, men also kill animals for no other purpose than pleasure. In addition, many are killed for the value of their skins, tusks, or other body parts. In many areas man hunts animals for reasons other than needing food. Is it not a crime to hunt animals needlessly—and an even bigger crime if the species is rare? Can a reasoning individual really feel happy because he has killed something or someone?

In contrast to this earthly spirit of hatred, revenge, and selfish killing, the spirit of heaven is love and forgiveness. Christ came to help us be reconciled to God and to men. Love takes away the hatred which motivates the murderer. But God's love does not sacrifice justice.

"One of Christ's last commands to His disciples was

'Love one another as I have loved you.' John 13:34. Do we obey this command, or are we indulging sharp, un-Christlike traits of character? If we have in any way grieved or wounded others, it is our duty to confess our fault and seek for reconciliation. This is an essential preparation that we may come before God in faith, to ask His blessing.''[21]

One human frame of mind constantly looks for the negative everywhere, with constant suspicion of other's motives and a tendency to make a mountain out of every small fault. But the essence of the inward law is to minimize such blemishes or stumblings and to give others the benefit of the doubt. Seeking and seeing the best in every person and situation is the prevailing disposition of those constrained by the inward law.

"Ye have heard that it hath been said, Thou shalt love thy neighbour, and hate thine enemy. But I say unto you, Love your enemies, bless them that curse you, do good to them that hate you, and pray for them which despitefully use you, and persecute you.''[22] "We are to love our enemies with the same love that Christ manifested toward His enemies by giving His life to save them.''[23]

"The heart in which love rules will not be filled with passion or revenge, by injuries which pride and self-love would deem unbearable. Love is unsuspecting, ever placing the most favorable construction upon the motives and acts of others. Love will never needlessly expose the faults of others. It does not listen eagerly to unfavorable reports, but rather seeks to bring to mind some good qualities of the one defamed.''[24]

Many of us seem to think that though we can love God, we cannot love our fellowmen. Yet the apostle John directly relates our love for God to the love we show those whose lives we touch day by day.[25] This is because love is a principle—when it is Christian love—and more than a feeling. We cannot generate it within ourselves or will it into existence by some form of meditation or self-analysis. The cross of Jesus is the greatest revelation of true love. Responding to that revelation creates an echo of that love in us—for all mankind.

"Pure love has special efficacy to do good, and can do nothing but good. It prevents discord and misery, and brings the truest happiness."[26] In this world of suspicion and hatred between races, classes, nations, business rivals, and even between husband and wife, the only real cure is love.

Once to a certain lawyer Jesus told a story about a man who was robbed and beaten on the way to Jericho. The wounded man's own countrymen passed by and paid no attention. But a Samaritan had sympathy on him and did everything he could to bring relief and comfort to the robbed and beaten Jew.

In God's love, our lives become complete. Not only is the quality of life greatly improved, but the length of life is also extended into eternity. In Christ, we have everlasting life. And in Christ, we may go to sleep in death awaiting His call to us to awaken once again. And if our life is his with Christ in God, we shall—when Christ appears here—also appear with Him in glory.[27]

"In our Saviour the life that was lost through sin is restored; for He has life in Himself to quicken whom He will. He is invested with the right to give immortality. The life that He laid down in humanity, He takes up again, and gives to humanity."[28] "The same power that raised Christ from the dead will raise His church, and glorify it with Christ as His bride."[29]

1. Genesis 2:7.
2. Ellen G. White, *Medical Ministry*, p. 7.
3. Acts 17:24, 25, RSV.
4. Ellen G. White, *Patriarchs and Prophets*, p. 522.
5. Ellen G. White, *The Ministry of Healing*, p. 113.
6. Ellen G. White Comments, *S.D.A. Bible Commentary*, vol. 1, p. 1081.
7. Matthew 5:21, 22.
8. John 10:10.
9. Ellen G. White, *Testimonies*, vol. 5, p. 17.
10. See Deuteronomy 19; Ellen G. White, *Patriarchs and Prophets*, pp. 515-517.
11. Numbers 35:30.
12. Genesis 9:6.
13. Numbers 35:31-33.
14. Exodus 21:14.
15. Exodus 20:13.

16. Ellen G. White, *Patriarchs and Prophets*, p. 308.
17. Ellen G. White Comments, *S.D.A. Bible Commentary*, vol. 2, p. 999.
18. Ellen G. White, *Patriarchs and Prophets*, p. 77.
19. Ellen G. White Comments, *S.D.A. Bible Commentary*, vol. 3, p. 1159.
20. Ellen G. White, *Patriarchs and Prophets*, p. 651.
21. Ellen G. White, *Christ's Object Lessons*, p. 144.
22. Matthew 5:43, 44.
23. Ellen G. White, *Medical Ministry*, 253.
24. Ellen G. White, *Testimonies*, vol. 5, pp. 168, 169.
25. See 1 John 4:12, 20.
26. Ellen G. White, *Testimonies*, vol. 4, p. 138.
27. Colossians 3:3, 4.
28. Ellen G. White, *The Desire of Ages*, pp. 786, 787.
29. Ellen G. White, *Selected Messages*, bk. 1, p. 305.

The Sacredness of Marriage

Seeing that "it is not good that the man should be alone,"[1] God made a companion for the man and pronounced them husband and wife. The creator intended that they form a union and "be one flesh."[2] This was God's original plan.

Marriage is a special opportunity for the outworking of the inward law. In order to make marriage successful, strong love must exist between husband and wife. Without love there can be no true marriage. True marriage is more than a physical union of two individuals. It is more than having children, more than sharing food and shelter. True marriage means a profound commitment to the welfare of the one's spouse, a deep desire to share and enjoy life together and to preserve a fidelity which cannot be violated.

Since marriage means sharing life together, meeting career goals, raising children, and spending the years of old age together, it can become a very complex relationship. Without strong mutual love, husband and wife—who often differ in heritage, temperament, and interests—may disagree and be led to serious clashes.

Everyone needs the fellowship of a companion. Everyone needs to talk to someone, to love someone, and be loved by someone. That is why "the Lord God said, It is not good that the man should be alone; I will make him an help meet for him."[3] In sickness, in failure, or in sadness, one needs someone who will sympathize and encourage. Even in success or in happiness, one needs someone to share that joy in order to be truly joyous. In order to safeguard the health of adults and children, preserve law and order in society, and provide a safe environment for the young, the institution of marriage was established. Although sin has robbed marriage of some of its original joy and purpose, marriage still lies at the foundation of the family and society; and it serves to preserve the purity and happiness of the race.

"He [Christ] announced to the world that marriage when kept pure and undefiled is a sacred institution."[4] "Around every family there is a sacred circle that should be kept unbroken. Within this circle no other person has a right to come. Let not the husband or the wife permit another to share the confidences that belong solely to themselves."[5]

The love relation between husband and wife is to be deepened as they live their lives together, meet problems together, and enjoy life's blessings together. This love has to be more than just physical. Married love envisions a total union of mind and purpose that can be fully achieved only after years of mutual self-giving.

"To gain a proper understanding of the marriage relation is the work of a lifetime. Those who marry enter a school from which they are never in this life to be graduated.

"However carefully and wisely marriage may have been entered into, few couples are completely united when the marriage ceremony is performed. The real union of the two in wedlock is the work of the afteryears."[6]

Most problems between husband and wife derive from differences in expectations. Being imperfect ourselves, we should not expect perfection on the part of our spouse. Once in China the emperor asked the elderly head of a big family, how his family, with over 100 members, could live so peacefully with one another. His answer consisted of only one word, *patience*, written 100 times. Even his living room was called the "Hall of the One Hundred Patiences."

Marriage relations can be very complicated. While the church discourages its members from marrying nonmembers, since problems may develop because of differences in religious convictions, the relations between an unbelieving spouse and a new convert constitute an altogether different situation.

In countries where tribal custom accepts polygamy, there are still other factors to consider. The church cannot encourage polygamy, but attempting to change long-established custom calls for much wisdom, patience, and prayer.

"To the rest speak I, not the Lord: If any brother hath a wife that believeth not, and she be pleased to dwell with him, let him not put her away. And the woman which hath an husband that believeth not, and if he be pleased to dwell with her, let her not leave him. For the unbelieving husband is sanctified by the wife, and the unbelieving wife is sanctified by the husband: else were your children unclean; but now are they holy.[7]

Paul advises that the believing spouse should work to help the unbelieving partner accept Christ and unite the whole family in Jesus. Patience and love will often win, and innocent children will not then be left to cope with the stresses of a divided home.

The converted spouse is charged with the responsibility of loving faithfulness. "He who has entered the marriage relation while unconverted is by his conversion placed under stronger obligation to be faithful to his companion, however widely they may differ in regard to religious faith; yet the claims of God should be placed above every earthly relationship, even though trials and persecution may be the result. With the spirit of love and meekness, this fidelity may have an influence to win the unbelieving one."[8]

"If the wife is an unbeliever and an opposer, the husband cannot, in view of the law of God, put her away on this ground alone. In order to be in harmony with the law of Jehovah, he must abide with her unless she chooses of herself to depart. He may suffer opposition and be oppressed and annoyed in many ways; he will find his comfort and his strength and support from God, who is able to give grace for every emergency. He should be a man of pure mind, of truly decided, firm principles, and God will give him wisdom in regard to the course which he should pursue. Impulse will not control his reason, but reason will hold the lines of control in her firm hand, that lust shall be held under bit and bridle."[9]

The only basis the Bible recognizes for divorce is adultery. Paul defines adultery in this way: "The woman which hath an husband is bound by the law to her husband so long as he liveth; but if the husband be dead, she is loosed from the law of her husband. So then if, while her husband liveth, she be married to another man, she shall be called an adulteress: but if her husband be dead, she is free from that law; so that she is no adulteress, though she be married to another man."[10]

Although Paul is here using the law of marriage as an illustration of the relationship of a believer to Christ and the law, he provides also a correct portrayal of the marriage relationship and properly defines adultery—a breakdown of the exclusive physical and spiritual oneness of a husband and wife. But Jesus sets what may seem an even more demanding standard. "But I say unto you, That whosoever looketh on a woman to lust after her hath committed adultery with her already in his heart"[11]

In this age of permissiveness and heavy emphasis on sex, temptations are ever present. We are all too prone to yield to them. God's people must be ever conscious of God's presence. Only the sense of being continually before God, of being surrounded by an atmosphere of holiness, can save us from falling into sin.

With more and more wives working outside the home and with increasing demands by some women for every type of "equality" with men, the stresses on the marriage relationship are greater now than ever. Increasingly, sexual favors are expected of women who hold certain jobs and positions. Some rights and freedoms have been interpreted as guarantees of license without penalty—as far as society goes. But there is an inward law—a higher law—that will demand fearsome penalties in the end. He or she who is unfaithful to a spouse soon knows not whom to trust. And trust is the bedrock of marriage.

Throughout much of the Old Testament era, understanding of and adherence to the seventh commandment was usually limited to adultery as a physical act. Both Jesus Christ and the apostle Paul amplified this commandment as including even adulterous motives and desires.

King David committed the crime of taking Uriah's wife. But later his repentance was genuine, and God did not order him to put away Bethseba. In New Testament times, as more light was given, the standard of Christian morality was elevated. Polygamy, frequently practiced in the Old Testament times, was now clearly forbidden. Premarital sex was also clearly forbidden. The highest ideal was upheld—there should be complete and undivided love between husband and wife.

Divorce is often the end results of a gradual alienation of mind, body, and spirit. Two once loving persons who exchanged marriage vows before the Lord have come to the point of parting—the result of a loss of love. At first the partners may not even realize that they are drifting apart. Regular periods of overtime work, frequent long trips away from home, excessive club obligations, lack of shared activities, or a thousand other factors may conspire to pull two persons apart. Suddenly one day they find that their love for each other is almost gone. And unless they take steps to reinvest in each other, their marriage may not survive.

Yet even if the fervor of the first love fades, like a piece of white paper that yellows with age, it is possible for two partners to restore happiness to their marriage and make it work again. Even if one falls into adultery, so long as the guilty one truly is repentant and determined to be faithful from then on, the other partner can choose to forgive. The mending of such a marriage may still be better than a divorce.

"The marriage covenant is sacred, but what an amount of lust and crime it covers! Those who feel at liberty, because married to degrade their bodies by beastly indulgence of the animal passions, will have their degraded course perpetuated in their children."[12]

We are all sadly aware that even among the saints, separation and divorce have multiplied. In order to avoid headaches and heartaches, young people should be very careful in choosing their life companions. They should seek counsel from their parents, their pastor, and other qualified counselors. How much the youth need to discover that true love is more a principle than an emotion!

The church is increasingly afflicted with the world's great rush to the divorce courts. Some say that divorce is more realistic than requiring partners to suffer on in a no-love-left situation. Others feel that many poor judgments are made as to the innocence or guilt of parties in separation and divorce cases.

When problems develop in a marriage, restraint, patience, and a spirit of forgiveness must be exercised. Even if a couple feels that there is very little to be salvaged from their marriage, a divorce that may leave scars on the children should only be considered as a last resort.

Early economic independence, a social trend emphasizing greater individuality, and a proportionate decrease in the influence of relatives and friends have each contributed to an atmosphere in which young couples today feel strongly that the affairs of their marriages are exclusively their own business. While this is true in some aspects, a husband and wife nevertheless do not live in isolation. They still live in a network of relatives and friends. Any tragedy befalling them causes sadness and heartache to children, parents, other relatives, and friends. They too feel the hurt, loneliness, and loss. Therefore the husband and wife do not have the right to do what they will with their marriage, without considering others. Just as a madman does not have a right to burn down his house, thereby endangering the neighborhood, a husband and wife do not automatically have the right to throw away their relationship without taking into consideration the impact of their decision upon others.

The counsel of parents, brothers, sisters, pastors, or marriage counselors should be sought. A cooling-off period should be allowed, and all the pros and cons should be weighed before any decision as serious as divorce is made. Just as the choice of a life partner is a serious matter, the decision to divorce is also serious—and all the more because the scars will take a long time to heal. In many cases, even a lifetime does not bring complete healing.

"A woman may be legally divorced from her husband by the laws of the land and yet not divorced in the sight of God and according to the higher law. There is only one sin, which is adultery, which can place the husband or wife in a position where they can be free from the marriage vow in the sight of God. Although the laws of the land may grant a divorce, yet they are husband and wife still in the Bible light, according to the laws of God."[13]

"To live with one who has broken the marriage vows and is covered all over with the disgrace and shame of guilty love, and realizes it not, is an eating canker to the soul; and yet a divorce is a lifelong, heartfelt sore."[14]

The causes of divorce are too many and too complex to be explored here. While we cannot sanction sin, we must not forget to love the sinners. We must not judge as though God has put us on the seat of final judgment. Church standards must be respected: and though there may be problems too complex to be resolved within church standards, we should do our best not to cause unnecessary sorrow.[15]

"Among the Jews a man was permitted to put away his wife for the most trivial offenses, and the woman was then at liberty to marry again. This practice led to great wretchedness and sin. In the Sermon on the Mount Jesus declared plainly that there could be no dissolution of the marriage tie, except for unfaithfulness to the marriage vow. 'Everyone,' He said. 'that putteth away his wife, saving for the cause of fornication, maketh her an adultress: whosoever shall marry her when she is put away committeth adultery.' ''[16]

Although marriage was the original arrangement for families and homes as the foundation of society, there are many in the church today who choose not to marry. And the church is becoming increasingly aware of the growing number of single people within its ranks. The Bible has every respect for such a life-style and notes the special contributions which the unmarried can make to the work of the gospel.[17]

To remain single is an option, but to marry is not a sin.[18] To marry or not is largely a matter of personal choice. Yet in many parts of the world, women strongly outnumber men in the Seventh-day Adventist Church, as in society as a whole. And as one dedicated dean of women once said of the young men of her earlier acquaintance: ''The acceptable were not available, and the available were not acceptable!'' Relatives, friends, and the church community have no reason to ridicule, condemn, or ostracize those who choose or happen to be single. Instead, activities appealing to the single adults in the church should be provided. And greater study must be given to the special contributions they can make to the fulfillment of the gospel commission.

Adventists must not take either marriage or singleness lightly. For it is from good families that many good church members of tomorrow come, whether they have a single parent or married parents. Parents should set good examples for their children. And the church must do everything possible to educate younger members to resolve that in marriage they will establish homes where the love of Christ rules. The church also has much to learn about the effective roles to be played by single members in families and in society. For God is the only safeguard of the integrity of today's family.

Unless one is totally dedicated to a worthy task and utterly immersed in it, to have a compatible, loving companion has many advantages.

"Jesus did not enforce celibacy upon any class of men. He came not to destroy the sacred relationship of marriage, but to exalt it and restore it to its original sanctity. He looks with pleasure upon the family relationship where sacred and unselfish love bears sway."[19]

"Husbands, love your wives, even as Christ also loved the church, and gave himself for it." "Wives, submit yourselves unto your own husbands, as unto the Lord."[20]

"Only let a woman realize that she is appreciated by her husband and is precious to him, not merely because she is useful and convenient in his house, but because she is a part of himself, and she will respond to his affection and reflect the love bestowed upon her. Let your wife be the object of your special and hearty attention. When you feel as God would have you, you will feel lost without the society of your wife."[21]

Even in this age of vaunted "rights" there are still marriages in which all the rights are on one side. The result is that the wife is made a servant to the passions and demands of her husband. Her needs and rights are all too often not even considered, let alone respected. Love will not manifest itself in self-indulgence—gratifying self at the expense of another.[22]

To one arbitrary father and husband this counsel was given: "Your wife needs tenderness and love. The Lord loves her. She is much nearer the kingdom of heaven than you. But she is dying by inches, and you are the one who is slowly taking her life. You can make her life happy if you will. You can encourage her to lean upon your large affections, to confide in you and love you."[23]

Of another man of cold disposition it was said: "Every word of tenderness, every word of appreciation and affectionate encouragement, will be remembered by her [his wife] and will reflect back in blessings upon her husband. . . . It will not be weakness or a sacrifice of manhood and dignity to give his wife expressions of tenderness and sympathy in words and acts."[24]

1. Genesis 2:18.
2. Genesis 2:24.
3. Genesis 2:18.
4. Ellen G. White, *The Adventist Home*, p. 341.
5. Ellen G. White, *The Ministry of Healing*, p. 361.
6. Ellen G. White, *The Adventist Home*, p. 105.
7. 1 Corinthians 7:12-14.
8. Ellen G. White, *The Adventist Home*, p. 69.
9. Ellen G. White, *The Adventist Home*, p. 344, 345.
10. Romans 7:2, 3.
11. Matthew 5:28.
12. Ellen G. White, *Testimonies*, vol. 2, p. 391.
13. Ellen G. White, *The Adventist Home*, p. 344.
14. Ellen G. White, *The Adventist Home*, p. 346.
15. See 2 Corinthians 2:5-8.
16. Ellen G. White, *Thoughts From the Mount of Blessing*, p. 63
17. Compare Matthew 19:10-12; Daniel 1; 1 Corinthians 7:7, 8.
18. See 1 Corinthians 7:26-28, RSV.
19. Ellen G. White, *The Adventist Home*, p. 121.
20. Ephesians 5:25, 22.
21. Ellen G. White, *Testimonies*, vol. 2, pp. 416, 417.
22. See Ellen G. White, *The Adventist Home*, p. 260.
23. Ellen G. White, *Testimonies*, vol. 2, p. 260.
24. Ellen G. White, *Testimonies*, vol. 3, pp. 530, 531.

The Possibility of Absolute Honesty

Honesty is a willingness and determination to stay with the truth. We trust people because we think they are honest. If there were no longer any honesty in the hearts of men, there could be no mutual trust. Just as a witness in court is required to tell "the truth, the whole truth, and nothing but the truth," so should we Christians tell only the truth in our words and deeds.

Jesus Christ was totally honest. When He felt sorrow over Jerusalem, He cried. When He saw merchants changing money and selling in the temple, He expressed His disapproval and righteous anger. When He was put on trial, He would not utter a single dishonest word to exonerate Himself. What He said reveals the truth of the universe, of the natural world, and of the spiritual world. Often He said, "Verily, verily, I say unto you." Here, *verily* means "truly" or "amen." He is the "Amen, the faithful and true witness."[1] "We utter the Amen through him, to the glory of God."[2]

We may agree with the wise man when he said, "Whoso keepeth his mouth and tongue keepeth his soul from troubles."[3] But can any human being be absolutely honest? Once God asked Satan, the great deceiver, "Hast thou considered my servant Job, that there is none like him in the earth, a perfect and an upright man, one that feareth God, and escheweth evil?"[4] Later, in tribulation, "Job did not sin with his lips."[5] Of how many men on earth could God say the same? Aren't we all men with "unclean lips, . . . [who] dwell in the midst of a people of unclean lips?"[6]

Since speech reflects the thoughts and feelings of a person—even more readily perhaps than do actions—man is frequently found at fault through his language. Yet if he is deceitful, even his nonverbal language may betray him. The discrepancy between a person's words and his body language may witness to his dishonesty.

We frequently flatter ourselves that we are not speaking falsely because we have couched our thoughts in words which sound above reproach. But there are a multitude of ways to bear false witness. The real heart of the matter lies in our intention. If we intend to deceive, we are guilty of deception, no matter how technically true our words are.

One may lie without uttering a word. One may lie by shrugging the shoulders or by signing a false document. Then again, many people lie by gossiping. They repeat what they hear and add to it.

We have heard from grade school days the story of the boy who cried, "Wolf, wolf"—a story of simple dishonesty. Today dishonesty may take more sophisticated forms, but it is still the same basic evil. Cheating is a widespread form of dishonesty. We see it in school examinations, in the filling out of tax forms, in the breaching of contracts, in the betraying of marriage vows, and in the forging of diplomas, paper money, identity cards, or passports.

Many love to tell tall tales. We may lie by exaggeration, by flattery, or by intentionally minimizing or suppressing truth.

"All lightness and trifling is positively forbidden in the word of God. His [the minister's] conversation should be in heaven, his words seasoned with grace. All flattery should be put away, for it is Satan's work to flatter. Poor, weak, fallen men generally think enough of themselves and need no help in this direction. Flattering your ministers is out of place. It perverts the mind and does not lead to meekness and humility; yet men and women love to be praised, and it is too frequently the case that ministers love it. Their vanity is gratified by it, but it has proved a curse to many. Reproof is more to be prized than flattery."[7]

It is a poor cause that requires flattery to win its way. Truth can stand up under test and scrutiny. Tragedy is compounded when men of intelligence, professing godliness, stoop to using flattery to achieve their ends. And it is equally lamentable when men of experience and in positions of highest trust surrender their better judgment and accept the distorted wooings of a flattering tongue.

Why do people lie? Why do people tell evil things about others? Why do people rationalize their own errors or failures? Certainly not from pure and holy motives. The absence of love prompts them to do so.

The world is so full of lies that, unless we are careful, we may lie unintentionally. Neighbors lie to us about their feelings and about the state of their health. Doctors lie to patients in the hope of "comforting" them. Ministers lie to their counselees for the purpose of alleviating their tensions so that they will not be so burdened by guilt feelings. Superstitious Chinese housewives even offer their kitchen gods sticky, sweet rice just before the New Year so that these gods, with their mouths full of sticky rice, will not be able to give a full report to the heavenly gods on wastefulness in the home. Even though we all know the truth, we nevertheless sometimes thoughtlessly bend the truth.

In the Orient, the bereaved are supposed to express their grief by crying out loud. When they get too tired to cry, they hire mourners to cry for them (as in Bible times). On the other hand, in the West the bereaved often attempt to restrain and conceal their true emotions. While both are extremes, the behavior code of society dictates in both cases the expected actions and responses.

Some people talk before they think. They may not be sure of what they want, but as they listen to themselves, their ideas are sorted out, their purposes clarified, and their determination strengthened. Thus the little tongue becomes the controller and the helm of the whole person.

"Lucifer himself had not at first been acquainted with the real nature of his feelings; for a time he had feared to express the workings and imaginings of his mind; yet he did not dismiss them. He did not see whither he was drifting."[8] His pride and ambition forbade him to repent—to take back his words. So he misled the angels with deception, and under the power of a lie he led Adam and Eve to disobey the law of God. From that time on he was a perpetual deceiver and liar.

Likewise, King Herod was caught by his words and so beheaded John the Baptist.[9] His pride prohibited him from repenting, and he became the slave of his own tongue. Numerous other individuals have experienced the same struggle. If the tongue is not controlled, its work will ruin a person.

According to an old English saying, "practice makes perfect." That may prove true at times. But even more certain is that practice makes permanent. We can come to accept our own lies as the truth if we repeat them often enough. We don't have to go very far back in history to find examples of this among national leaders of our own day.

Words can kill. We look with loathing upon the cannibal but hardly ever stop to think that our words may similarly consume another's character.

"We think with horror of the cannibal who feasts on the still warm and trembling flesh of his victim; but are the results of even this practice more terrible than are the agony and ruin caused by misrepresenting motive, blackening reputation, dissecting character? Let the children, and the youth as well, learn what God says about these things: 'Death and life are in the power of the tongue.' Proverbs 18:21."[10]

Note James's forceful words in his portrayal of the human tongue: "The tongue can no man tame; it is an unruly evil, full of deadly poison."[11]

Sometimes we allow our tongues unbridled freedom before the mind awakes to the trouble stirred up. "Some talk too much; they stand in this position: 'Report, . . . and we will report it.' Miserable indeed is such a position! If all these gossipers would ever bear in mind that an angel is following them, recording their words, there would be less talking and much more praying."[12]

"Words have kindled fires that have been hard to quench. They have also brought joy and gladness to many souls. And when words are spoken because God says, 'Speak unto them My words,' they often cause sorrow unto repentence."[13]

The psalmist recognized the great need for tongue discipline and expressed his desire to exercise control. "I will take heed to my ways, that I sin not with my tongue: I will keep my mouth with a bridle, while the wicked is before me."[14]

He who lies for personal gain may evade detection for a time and feel that his new prosperity justifies the means. But if he continues on this course, he becomes a perpetual liar, for eventually he has to lie again to cover his first lies. If he does not get caught in the meshes of his own web of falsehoods, he soon finds himself in a more desperate plight. Knowing the depth of his deception of others, he comes to trust the word of no one himself.

Since the tongue is so difficult to control, we may feel that the offending organ should be excised to keep ourselves honest. But does this really solve the basic problem of dishonesty? If it does, then the dumb may be in better standing before God!

Being honest or being dishonest can become a matter of habit. We have noticed that an actor, after having acted a certain role for a period of time, often finds it hard to drop that role. The role has molded his behavior for too long to be dropped easily.

Likewise, if we practice dishonesty for a period of time, we will find it difficult to break that habit. One indulgence in dishonesty paves the way for a second, and each time it becomes easier. It takes a high level of spiritual alertness to discern the subtlety of Satan in trapping us in his snares. And it takes a constant sense of the abiding presence of Christ to remain above the temptation.

"Divers weights, and divers measures, both of them are alike abomination to the Lord." "Divers weights are an abomintion to the Lord; and a false balance is not good."[15]

An honest God hates double standards. Not uncommonly a dishonest merchant will use two different scales—one for buying and one for selling. Thus he makes a profit by cheating. But double standards are not only to be found in business. They enter into all areas of human relationships. Yet the Bible counsel is that "whatsoever you would that men should do to you, do ye even so to them."[16]

A man cannot serve two gods at the same time. In some way he is more loyal to one than to the other. Likewise, the tongue shows a person's loyalty. By blessing God and others, a man shows his allegiance to God. But by cursing he demonstrates his allegiance to Satan.

Those who suffer the psychological problem commonly called split personality often behave as though they were two different people. Those who curse and bless with the same mouth exhibit similar symptoms. Only when one fully submits himself to the influence of the Holy Spirit can he be free of this divided allegiance.

"The mixture of cursing with the blessing may suggest the insincerity of the blessing (cf. Prov. 18:21). . . . James appeals to the fellowship of believers in Christ and to the unity found in the fatherhood of God. . . . Though some of the church members to whom James writes are guilty of cursing men while blessing God, he still regards them with affection."[17]

"Of all the gifts which God has given to man, none is more noble or a greater blessing than the gift of speech, if it is sanctified by the Holy Spirit. It is with the tongue we convince and persuade; with it we offer prayer and praise to God; and with it we convey rich thoughts of the Redeemer's love."[18]

Words can condemn and kill, yet they also encourage and give life. How important it is that we not sin with our lips but use our speech instead to reveal the happiness of an honest heart where Jesus Christ rules as the Lord.

Motivated by such negative feelings as pride, jealousy, shame, hatred, or greed, one may misuse the gift of speech to accuse, insinuate, or falsify. "If ye have bitter envying strife in your hearts, glory not, and lie not against the truth. This wisdom descendeth not from above, but is earthly, sensual, devilish."[19]

We must be on guard as to what controls our minds. "The tongue is evil only when it is controlled by a mind motivated by the forces of evil. When a man does not let the Holy Spirit control his thoughts, and thus his speech, the tongue functions as an instrument of evil."[20]

Even a tongue controlled by the Holy Spirit, however, may speak words that result in strife. "He who is truly wise seeks to avoid quarrels and strife, but his desire for peace will not keep him from presenting the truth, even though trouble may result. Jesus predicted that the proclamation of truth would bring contention into the world, . . . but the resulting strife is the fault of those who oppose the truth, not of those who wisely present it. Purity of life and doctrine must never be sacrificed in an effort to secure peace."[21]

According to the apostle Paul, we are to make sustained efforts to live peacefully with all men.[22] Yet in defending truth, we cannot completely avoid confrontations. Nonetheless, we must not be overcome by a spirit of strife. We must be all the more earnest in seeking God's grace that He may deliver us from evil. Even under great pressure, divine grace is sufficient for us. We are promised that we will be given words of wisdom when we are brought to the court of judgment. If we are willing to place ourselves under the influence of the Holy Spirit, He can control our tongues and help us gain the victory over undisciplined speech.

The Bible says of a man that "as he thinketh in his heart, so is he."[23] If one's mind is filled with peace, gentleness, kindness, and honesty, his speech will reveal his heart.

When a group of men engage in conversation, it does not take long for the group to identify the scholar, the farmer, or the former sailor among them. The vocabulary, the sentence structure, the expletives betray their identities.

Of course, to be honest does not mean to tell everything one knows to everybody everywhere. There is "a time to weep, and a time to laugh," "a time to keep silence, and a time to speak."[24] In order to be absolutely honest, one must feel that he is constantly in the presence of God. Whatever he says and does will be recorded in heaven. He must be willing to uphold the principle of honesty to the point of sacrifice. Let us pray for wisdom from above that we may be honest in motive and perfect in language—according to the inward law.

1. Revelation 3:14.
2. 2 Corinthians 1:20, RSV.
3. Proverbs 21:23.
4. Job 1:8.
5. Job 2:10, RSV.
6. Isaiah 6:5.
7. Ellen G. White, *Testimonies*, vol. 2, p. 338.
8. Ellen G. White, *Patriarchs and Prophets*, p. 39.
9. See Matthew 14:1-12.
10. Ellen G. White, *Education*, p. 235.
11. James 3:8.
12. Ellen G. White, *Testimonies*, vol. 4, p. 40.
13. Ellen G. White Comments, *S.D.A. Bible Commentary*, vol. 3, p. 1142.
14. Psalm 39:1.
15. Proverbs 20:10, 23.
16. Matthew 7:12.
17. *S.D.A. Bible Commentary*, vol. 7, p. 527.
18. Ellen G. White, *Testimonies to Ministers*, p. 316.
19. James 3:14, 15.
20. *S.D.A. Bible Commentary*, vol. 7, p. 526.
21. *S.D.A. Bible Commentary*, vol. 7, p. 529.
22. See Romans 12:18.
23. Proverbs 23:7.
24. Ecclesiastes 3:4, 7.

The Root of All Evil

Covetousness was involved in the first sin. Lucifer became Satan because he coveted the position and glory of Christ, which could never have been his. Eve sinned because she coveted beauty, intelligence, and knowledge.

From covetousness is derived pride, theft, dishonesty, adultery, murder, and many other kinds of sin and crime. Covetousness—along with dishonesty—is perhaps the most widely committed sin. Some people covet material things; others covet fame. Still others covet position and power.

"The love of money is the root of all evil: which while some coveted after, they have erred from the faith, and pierced themselves through with many sorrows."[1] While money itself is not evil, the *love* of money is the root of all evil. The covetous motive still leads one to steal, in violation of the inward law of love.

To want to enjoy better things is natural. While a desire for better things is not sin, if one nurtures that desire to the extent that he reckons things as being more important than God, he has created an idol for himself. If he wants something so badly that he gets it through illegitimate means, he is stealing.

Wherever money is in circulation, people love money. Besides material things, money can bring to its possessor fame, power, and influence. To many people, especially those in the capitalistic world, money is the standard for measuring success. Success means a bigger house, an efficient car (or many cars), a fat bank balance, and conspicuous consumption of life's delicacies.

A Chinese adage says, "Money can make the devil run the stonemill." Because money is so useful, the pursuit of it has for many become all-consuming.

Covetousness means craving for something other persons have. If this desire is not brought under control, it will become the dominant motive of all behavior.

In the pursuit of money, one may become oblivious to those in need around him—the sick, the elderly, the poor, the handicapped, and the orphans that can be found in every community. However, the responsibility for caring for these unfortunate ones rests increasingly upon the community, because in one way or another they are often the products of our changing society— the victims of so-called progress.

When money is used for philanthropic purposes, it can help fight disease, alleviate poverty, and promote education and culture. When put to illegal uses, money corrupts and creates scandals even in the higher circles of governments.

Consider the rich young ruler who turned away from Jesus so sorrowfully when he heard the Master's reply to his sincere question, "What good thing shall I do, that I may have eternal life?"[2] This affluent young man had the desire to become a perfect man, but unfortunately he was addicted to money. The desire to keep his money was greater than the desire to enter everlasting life.

Note that "the Bible condemns no man for being rich, if he has acquired his riches honestly. Not money, but the love of money, is the root of all evil. . . . But many, absorbed in their interest in worldly treasures, become insensible to the claims of God and the needs of their fellow men."[3]

The rich young ruler, if seeking church membership today, would probably be warmly welcomed into the church. Young, rich, handsome, and well-educated, he had a good reputation and was exemplary in his conduct. What more could an evangelist expect from a baptismal candidate? But Jesus seemed to have made it unnecessarily difficult for him to be His follower. Does Jesus have different standards for different persons? No. The Bible says that Jesus loved him and told him to sell everything he had and follow Him. This the rich young ruler needed in order to cure his disease of love for money. As long as he loved money more than he loved Jesus, he could not be a real follower of Jesus. Jesus would not have occupied the throne in his heart.

Today Jesus requires us to return to Him, not everything we have, but only a tenth of what we have, along with freewill offerings. Even so, some find it a temptation to steal from God by not returning a faithful tithe. If we look at the value of money—what money can buy—and the material things which we enjoy, we find it difficult to let go of what we have, regardless of its value. But if we turn our eyes to Jesus to look at His love, to look at His glory, and to anticipate the happiness of eternal life, we find it easy to do whatever Jesus wants us to do. We may then return not only the tithe but perhaps even a second tithe or a third tithe, should it be possible for us to do so.

The time will come when money will be useless to us and useless in God's work. How important that we not allow covetousness to prevent us from using our money to save souls while it can still be used for such profitable ends.

The Bible says: "Ye have heaped treasure together for the last days. Behold, the hire of the labourers who have reaped down your fields, which is of you kept back by fraud, crieth: and the cries of them which have reaped are entered into the ears of the Lord of sabaoth."[4]

Here is a warning to the employer or manager who has kept back by fraud that which is due to his laborers or employees. The profits of a factory, company, or farm should be equitably shared by all who contribute to its success. Stockholders, managers, owners, and bosses do provide houses, goods, tools, equipment, capital, and management to make such success possible. But without the participation of the employees, there can be no profit. Owners and financiers must recognize the rights and proportionate share of the laborers. Some laborers may be unskilled, lazy, and irresponsible; but the mistakes of a few should not be made the reason to exploit the whole. Enlightened managers nowdays realize the need to share profits adequately and justly with the laborers.

Let us consider briefly three passages from the Bible that mention three different kinds of covetousness. The first is the parable recorded in Matthew 20:1-16. It describes a demand for equality. In effect the complainer was trying to breach his contract with the manager. Because other workers got a better deal, he became jealous of it. That is definitely a form of covetousness.

The second text is in Matthew 20:20-28 and records the request of a mother who wanted her two sons, James and John, to sit on either side of Christ when He became King. To hope, make plans, and work for the best for one's children is understandable. But to desire them to occupy positions not rightfully theirs, unsuited to their capabilities and qualifications, is another form of covetousness.

The third text, recorded in Luke 15:11-32, is the story of the prodigal son's request for his inheritance. In the Orient this kind of request for one's inheritance is considered as wishing for the father to die—a most disrespectful attitude and a very covetous act. Knowing this may provide added significance to one of the best-known of Christ's many parables.

Before commiting the crime of theft, one would first have harbored feelings of covetousness—a craving for that which he should not attempt to get, such as the possessions or the wife of his neighbor. However, keeping up with the Joneses has become a contagious disease. Further, the appetite for "things" is cultivated by the attractive but often deceitful advertising of the mass media.

When the love for material things increases, the love for honesty, reputation, and spiritual experience decreases. In a society which "despises the poor but not the prostitutes," as expressed in a Chinese saying, the ethical standards of some people are bound to be distorted.

Therefore, people don't feel guilty when they evade taxes, when they cheat in examinations, or even when they embezzle from the public or the organization for which they work. Some even develop the rationalization that society or the government owes them so much already that any cheating they do—personal long-distance phone calls at company expense, stealing of computer time, personal use of company stationery—is but restoring justice!

An extreme form of covetous behavior is shown in gambling—horse racing, casino attendance, poker games, mah-jongg, or the numbers game. Any kind of gambling has the purpose of gaining some undeserved benefit.

The gambler takes chances, and the excitement is habit-forming. Once a person is absorbed in gambling, he may lose all interest in working for a wage or a profit. Instead he often begins to believe in fate—in his "luck." Many gamblers rationalize and believe in some form of predestination. They are not satisfied with an ordinary life. Diligence, thrift, and hard work have no place in their lives. It doesn't take long for a gambler to degrade himself by becoming a pitiful parasite, preying on the generosity of society.

Perhaps similar to gambling may be short-term speculation in stocks or gold. Having contributed nothing to the economy, people become absorbed in speculation, hoping for a quick profit.

Others resort to tactics such as strikes to get higher pay. Still others would like to work fewer hours for more pay without increasing efficiency. On one hand, we should not condone practices whereby workers are not paid a just share of the total profit. But neither should we expect to work less and get more.

Of Lucifer it is written: "Thou hast said in thine heart, I will ascend into heaven, I will exalt my throne above the stars of God: I will sit also upon the mount of the congregation, in the sides of the north: I will ascend above the heights of the clouds; I will be like the most High."[5]

Lucifer clearly knew his position and his relationship with God. He was already the chief of angels; he was directly under God. Despite all the glory he had, he coveted the special position, power, and glory of Jesus Christ, who, as God, had been with the Father from all eternity. Somehow Satan forgot that he was a creature and not the Creator.[6] He coveted something that he was not and never could be, and that covetousness developed into a rebellion in heaven and led to the downfall of the first couple on this earth and all the resultant pain and death in this present world.

"Pride of position is a deep-seated evil which has ruined thousands. Yes, tens of thousands, full of ambition for distinction and display, have been ruined because they have lost sight of principle. They have measured themselves among themselves, and compared themselves with themselves. Their eager grasping for credit and reward has resulted in diminished spirituality. This is a lesson all should study carefully that they may be warned against selfishness and avarice, against pride which destroys love for God and corrodes the soul."[7]

"Whenever pride and ambition are indulged, the life is marred, for pride, feeling no need, closes the heart against the infinite blessings of Heaven. He who makes self-glorification his aim will find himself destitute of the grace of God, through whose efficiency the truest riches and the most satisfying joys are won."[8]

From time immemorial, people have worried. They worry over the security and growth of their money. Some worry about their health. They worry about what to eat and what to wear. For some, eating is more to them than nourishment. For them, eating means the right kind of food with the right kind of people in the right kind of social setting.

Some women, as well as some men, worry every day about what to wear. Some covet being something they are not. They have nonessential plastic surgery done, wear various wigs over their quite acceptable natural hair, make up their faces extravagantly, paint their fingernails and toenails, "starve" themselves to preserve "the figure," and wear garments that offend Christian sensibilities of modesty. All these activities reflect forms of covetousness.

If one is grateful to God for what He has given him, even the crippled person can accept his lot. With the hope and assurance that someday soon he will be given a perfect body, he does not need to covet being something which he is not.

"There are many whose hearts are aching under a load of care because they seek to reach the world's standard. . . . In order to gratify ambition and worldly desires, they wound the conscience, and bring upon themselves an additional burden of remorse. The continual worry is wearing out the life forces. Our Lord desires them to lay aside this yoke of bondage. . . . In every difficulty He has His way prepared to bring relief."[9]

In His Sermon on the Mount, Jesus gave this principle: "Seek ye first the kingdom of God, and his righteousness; and all these things shall be added unto you."[10]

Often the outworking of covetousness is stealing—prohibited in the eighth commandment: "Thou shalt not steal."[11] "Both public and private sins are included in the prohibition. The eighth commandment condemns manstealing and slave dealing, and forbids wars of conquest. It condemns theft and robbery. It demands strict integrity in the minutest details of the affairs of life. . . . It declares that every attempt to advantage oneself by the ignorance, weakness, or misfortune of another is registered as fraud in the books of heaven."[12]

If one forgets that he is but a steward of the Lord, he will claim as his own that which God has entrusted to him as a steward. He certainly will find it difficult to return to God the tithe, which is God's.[13] This attitude can lead one to cheat his fellowmen, the government, his customers, his wife, and just about everybody around him. Some people seem to find it impossible not to steal. To them, stealing is a compulsive behavior that they cannot seem to control. They even go around stealing from their friends or from the department store worthless little things that they do not need.

In the tenth commandment there is another item God forbids us to covet—a neighbor's wife. If one stole a cow, he could return it to its original owner. But if he stole his neighbor's marital partner, it would be hard, if not impossible to recompense the damage.

When we consider gamblers, tax evaders, shoplifters, and dishonest manufacturers and merchants, we may be surprised by the number of people who have violated the eight and tenth commandments.

Strict integrity includes the principle of restoration. Some things can never be fully repaid—such as stolen reputation or stolen affection—but most of them can and must be.

When one is elderly he should consider how his properties are to be managed after death. A Christian has a responsibility before God to prepare his will so that properties may not be given over to the government or even to children if it would be to their injury. If we acknowledge that our possessions are God's and we have the responsibility of using our means to advance His cause, then we should not close our ears to requests for funds to help the needy and to forward God's work. Negligence in preparing a will to direct the disposal of our properties may be a form of covetousness. As stewards of God's money, we should realize our responsibility not only while we are living, but even when we are no longer able to manage what God has entrusted to us.

"Being in the form of God, [Jesus] thought it not robbery to be equal with God: but made himself of no reputation, and took upon him the form of a servant, and was made in the likeness of men: and being found in fashion as a man, he humbled himself, and became obedient unto death, even the death of the cross."[14]

The opposite of covetousness is generosity, the giving of one's self in service to others. In this respect also, Jesus is our perfect Example. Instead of coming to rule as a king, He took upon Himself the form of a servant and was made in the likeness of men to live among the poor and to die for us willingly, as though He were a criminal. Such self-denial we have never seen in anyone else. Meditation upon this theme will prompt us to shout praises to Him and to love Him as we have never loved before.

Notice how we ought to consider the wealth in our hands. "Money is a trust from God. It is not ours to expend for the gratification of pride or ambition. In the hands of God's children it is food for the hungry, and clothing for the naked."[15]

God gives us the power to gain wealth.[16] The angels are "ministering spirits, sent forth to minister for them who shall be heirs of salvation."[17] In God's family everyone exists to serve others. By serving one another—through our means, our talents, our energies—we make the universe a paradise.

1. 1 Timothy 6:10.
2. Matthew 19:16.
3. Ellen G. White, *The Ministry of Healing*, p. 212.
4. James 5:3, 4.
5. Isaiah 14:13, 14.
6. See also Ezekiel 28:14-17.
7. Ellen G. White, *Selected Messages*, bk. 2, pp. 184, 185.
8. Ellen G. White, *Prophets and Kings*, p. 60.
9. Ellen G. White, *The Desire of Ages*, p. 330.
10. Matthew 6:33.
11. Exodus 20:15.
12. Ellen G. White, *Patriarchs and Prophets*, p. 308.
13. See Malachi 3:8.
14. Philippians 2:6-8.
15. Ellen G. White, *The Ministry of Healing*, p. 287.
16. Deuteronomy 8:18.
17. Hebrews 1:14.

Natural Law and Moral Law

Man is a part of God's total creation. Physical laws, which govern material things and affect the physical aspects of our body, and the moral law, which governs our conduct, are authored by the same God. Therefore, there is complete harmony between the two. Throughout history, some philosophers and religionists have advocated a theory of dualism—the physical versus the metaphysical, or the material versus the spiritual. Even today in this scientific age, there are still people who believe that a spiritual world is superimposed upon the physical world and that man is able to live in one world or the other or in both worlds without their affecting each other. Although such a theory defies logic and common sense, many people have accepted it without any question.

Only recently scientists have discovered the influence of the psychological functions of the mind on the physiological functions of the body, and vice versa. When God tells us that ''a merry heart doeth good like a medicine: but a broken spirit drieth the bones,''[1] This is an indication that nature—His second book—agrees with His first—the Bible.

The spirit of prophecy clearly states: ''The laws of nature are the laws of God—as truly divine as are the precepts of the Decalogue. The laws that govern our physical organism, God has written upon every nerve, muscle, and fiber of the body. Every careless or willful violation of these laws is a sin against our Creator. . . .

"The influence of the mind on the body, as well as the body on the mind, should be emphasized. The vital power of the brain, promoted by mental activity, energizes the whole system, and is thus an invaluable aid in resisting disease. This should be made plain. The power of the will and the importance of self-control, both in the preservation and in the recovery of health, the depressing and even ruinous effect of anger, discontent, selfishness, or impurity, and, on the other hand, the marvelous life-giving power to be found in cheerfulness, unselfishness, gratitude, should also be shown."[2]

"Transgression of physical law is transgression of the moral law; for God is as truly the author of physical laws as He is the author of the moral law. His law is written with His own finger upon every nerve, every muscle, every faculty, which has been entrusted to man. And every misuse of any part of our organism is a violation of that law."[3]

Since the human mind and the human body are the most wonderful of God's creation in this world, we should find the natural and the moral laws working intricately in us. While what we eat influences how we think, how we feel also influences what we are. Our physical health as well as our spiritual health depends upon the observance of God's laws, both natural and moral.

"The relation of the physical organism to the spiritual life is one of the most important branches of education. It should receive careful attention in the home and in the school. All need to become acquainted with their physical structure and the laws that control natural life."[4]

In Psalm 19, the psalmist categorically declares God to be the author of the two sets of laws—the natural (physical) and the moral. "The heavens declare the glory of God; and the firmament sheweth his handywork." "The law of the Lord is perfect, converting the soul: the testimony of the Lord is sure, making wise the simple."[5]

When God created our planet, part of His plan was the creation of man. Man is part of His total creation.

Since man's body is governed by natural law and his behavior by moral law, these two laws must reflect the harmonious will of their Author. Adam was created in God's image. Not only did he have high intelligence, a beautiful body, and extraordinary vitality; but he also reflected God's love. The motives of his behavior were good and pure, and he lived happily because, in perfect trust, he observed God's laws.

The natural laws were initially intended to interpret the spiritual ones. "The whole natural world is designed to be an interpreter of the things of God. To Adam and Eve in their Eden home, nature was full of the knowledge of God, teeming with divine instruction. To their attentive ears it was vocal with the voice of wisdom. Wisdom spoke to the eye and was received into the heart, for they communed with God in His created works.[6]

When God announced His moral law—the Ten Commandments—at Sinai, His presence, with all his power and majesty, caused an extraordinary physical phenomenon. "There were thunders and lightnings, and a thick cloud upon the mount, and the voice of the trumpet exceedingly loud; so that all the people that was in the camp trembled." "And mount Sinai was altogether on a smoke, because the Lord descended upon it in fire: and the smoke thereof ascended as a smoke of a furnace, and the whole mount quaked greatly."[7]

The fire, smoke, lightning, thunder, earthquake, and noise of trumpets created a frightening scene before the Israelites. The power of God was greatly manifested when He descended on Mount Sinai to announce His law. The power of nature and the power of law were demonstrated by the same Author. The reason for making the pronouncement solemn and memorable was to impress the minds of the Israelites with the importance of God's law. In Egypt many of them had forgotten God's law and the sacredness of it. To change that, something extraordinary and dramatic was needed.

However, when God speaks to man, He does not

usually appear in the fire or the earthquake. His voice is heard in quietness. The Holy Spirit may descend as tongues of fire, but only the "still small voice" gives us the understanding and faith which comes from His law. For His law is His will, His character, and His wisdom.

Our God is an orderly God. This aspect of His character is demonstrated in nature. "God said, Let the earth bring forth the living creature after his kind, cattle, and creeping things, and beast of the earth after his kind: and it was so."[8]

In this short verse is hidden the genesis of zoology, entomology, taxonomy, genetics, paleontology, and other disciplines of science. The short phrase "after his kind" governs the laws of genetics and rules out the possibility of a theory of evolution that denies the creatorship of God. Regardless of how one looks at nature, he cannot find enough convincing evidence to prove the evolutionary theory. God cannot contradict Himself.

Consider even the principles that controlled the miracles of Jesus: "The Saviour in His miracles revealed the power that is continually at work in man's behalf to sustain and to heal him. Through the agencies of nature, God is working, day by day, hour by hour, moment by moment, to keep us alive, to build up and restore us. . . . All life-giving power is from Him."[9]

Natural science is the knowledge of nature known to men. However, the total body of knowledge known to men today does not constitute all the knowledge of nature. Otherwise there could be no new discovery. When the Bible said, "When he [God] established the force of the wind and measured out the waters,"[10] few understood its true meaning until recently, when scientific knowledge expanded with explosive force.

We should be very grateful that God's natural laws do not change. If they did, we could not have any scientific knowledge. The law of gravity, the periodicity of the chemical elements, the quantum theory, the genetic laws, and a host of other natural laws remain the same century after century, millennium after millennium.

Otherwise we would not have been able to study science, and our own existence would have been in jeopardy.

If the laws of gravity changed from time to time, the measurement of weight, aerodynamics, and even the olympic records of high jumps would all be confused; and the erratic gravitational poles of the sun and moon would make the tide highly unstable and force 80 percent of the world's population—now living in the lowlands or coastal areas—to flee to the mountains. If the radiation of the sun increased by 1 percent, the change of the temperature on earth would melt enough snow in the polar regions to flood the whole earth. We could go on and on, demonstrating that we are very fortunate to live in a world governed by God's orderly and changeless natural laws.

"The dietary principles of Leviticus 11, together with other sanitary and health regulations, were intended by a wise Creator to promote health and longevity. . . . Based as they are upon the nature and requirements of the human body, these principles could in no way be affected either by the cross or by the disappearance of Israel as a nation. Principles that contributed to health 3,500 years ago will produce the same results today."[11]

Every increase in the amazing growth of scientific knowledge in our day only adds to our wonder over the intricate and unfailing laws under which God has placed every atom of His creation. Not one detail has escaped the attention of the divine mind and hand. But while everything in this creation, animate and inanimate, is under law, only man is under moral law. His intelligence and his capacity to distinguish right from wrong under divine tutelage make him responsible to this law. The conscience again is the agency or channel for this capacity, in a mind capable of finding the law holy, just, and good.

"God has given us His holy precepts, because He loves mankind. To shield us from the results of transgression, He reveals the principles of righteousness. The law is an expression of the thought of God; when received in Christ, it becomes our thought. It lifts us above the power of natural desires and tendencies, above temptations that lead to sin. God desires us to be happy, and He gave us the precepts of the law that in obeying them we might have joy. When at Jesus' birth the angels sang,—'Glory to God in the highest, and on earth peace, good will toward men' (Luke 2:14), they were declaring the principles of the law which He had come to magnify and make honorable."[12]

The wise man said "For as he thinketh in his heart, so is he."[13] This statement tells us that our thinking changes our whole being, including the body. One's thought, one's mood, and one's attitude dictate one's behavior and health.

Some Christians misunderstand the Bible and claim that the moral law was nailed to and nullified by the cross when Jesus was crucified. But Jesus Himself said, "Think not that I am come to destroy the law, or the prophets: I am not come to destroy, but to fulfill. For verily I say unto you, Till heaven and earth pass, one jot or one tittle shall in no wise pass from the law, till all be fulfilled."[14]

As natural law is changeless, so is God's moral law; for God's moral law is really the expression of His character—His love.

"While the Saviour's death brought to an end the law of types and shadows, it did not in the least detract from the obligation of the moral law. On the contrary, the very fact that it was necessary for Christ to die in order to atone for transgression of that law, proves it to be immutable."[15]

The laws which govern our health are also a part of God's total creation. If we live our lives according to the health laws laid down by God, then we have a better chance of enjoying good health and having a peaceful mind. The Lord said, "Know ye not that ye are the temple of God, and that the Spirit of God dwelleth in you? If any man defile the temple of God, him shall God destroy; for the temple of God is holy, which temple ye are."[16] "If thou wilt diligently hearken to the voice of the Lord thy God, and wilt do that which is right in his sight, and wilt give ear to his commandments, and keep all his statutes, I will put none of these diseases upon thee, which I have brought upon the Egyptians: for I am the Lord that healeth thee."[17]

"Health is a blessing of which few appreciate the value: yet upon it the efficiency of our mental and physical powers largely depends. Our impulses and passions have their seat in the body, and it must be kept in the best condition physically and under the most spiritual influences in order that our talents may be put to the highest use.

"Anything that lessens physical strength enfeebles the mind and makes it less capable of discriminating between right and wrong. We become less capable of choosing the good and have less strength of will to do that which we know to be right.

"The misuse of our physical powers shortens the period of time in which our lives can be used for the glory of God. And it unfits us to accomplish the work God has given us to do. By allowing ourselves to form wrong habits, by keeping late hours, by gratifying appetite at the expense of health, we lay the foundation for feebleness. By neglecting physical exercise, by overworking mind or body, we unbalance the nervous system."[18]

Sunshine, pure air, exercise, rest, wholesome food, and a peaceful mind are necessary to good health. But modern men are plagued by polluted air, physical inactivity, lack of sleep, tension, indulgence of appetite, and the use of drugs—including alcohol and tobacco. As we return to a more simple life, we can enjoy life more abundantly.

But it is easier to say this than to do it. We all tend to be slaves of our environment, our jobs, and our ambitions. It takes real determination and a strong will to change the pattern of our behavior. That is why some people pay hundreds of dollars to go to conditioning centers to have their pattern of behavior altered under the friendly advice of instructors.

However, not everyone can go away to another place to change his life. The change must begin at home. Members of the family must help one another and remind each other of the importance of adhering to health principles. We must be willing to earn fewer dollars, look for recreation instead of entertainment, and withdraw from frivolous social fraternization in order to have more time with the family, that the family may function as a personal health club. In so doing, the family will find it natural to stick together and to get closer to God.

"Life is a gift of God. Our bodies have been given us to use in God's service, and He desires that we shall care for and appreciate them. We are possessed of physical as well as mental faculties. Our impulses and passions have their seat in the body, and therefore we must do nothing that would defile this entrusted possession. Our bodies must be kept in the best possible condition physically, and under the most spiritual influences, in order that we may make the best use of our talents."[19]

The Lord said, "I am the Lord your God: ye shall therefore sanctify yourselves, and ye shall be holy; for I am holy."[20] The word *holy* connotes deepest reverence, spiritual purity, and sacredness—that which is set apart as different from things common or ordinary.

Following natural laws for good health in turn promotes a good conscience that works best under God's moral laws. Listen to this counsel: "The relation that exists between the mind and the body is very intimate. When one is affected, the other sympathizes. The condition of the mind affects the health to a far greater degree than many realize. Many of the diseases from which men suffer are the result of mental depression. Grief, anxiety, discontent, remorse, guilt, distrust, all tend to break down the life forces and to invite decay and death."[21]

Man was made as a whole person. The psychological and the physiological functions are interrelated. Many get sick and die because of a lack of desire to continue living. On the other hand, many cannot abstain from sinful habits because of their physical condition. An example is the cigarette smoker who knows the harmfulness of the cigarette but is unable to stop smoking. If one is plagued by disease and sin, in order to break the vicious circle, he must first return to God just as he is. His sins will be forgiven. Only then will he have the regenerated willpower to fight the forces of darkness.

When we see or hear about hale and hearty souls who have lived to be a hundred or more and learn that they have been lifelong smokers or drinkers or loose in their living, we cannot but wonder about the health principles we have been taught. How can one who indulges himself live so long when conscientious observers of every health rule suffer and perhaps die young? Are the health principles unsound? Are they only for those with a poor start in life?

Much might be said on this. But when it is said that we are all born equal, that does not apply to the physical endowment with which we enter life. Some are born more "equal" than others. On the other hand, a life of hard work can counter many of the ill effects of imbibing in the unhealthful. None of us knows exactly what our fate might have been had we lived differently. We can only surmise, based on the law of averages. But it is probable that the mind and soul are more easily affected by our physical habits than we will know in this life. Judgment and eternity will reveal many things. No follower of Jesus will choose to ignore the claims of the laws of health.

We often marvel today at the high achievements of the descendants of the ancient people of Israel. Undoubtedly the blessings of their forebearers have come down to them. Yet ancient Israel failed in a large measure to be to the world the savor of life unto life which Jehovah intended. She could have been the world's greatest object lesson in good health and every other advantage. What Daniel and his companions were in Babylon, Israel could have been in the world at large.

This may illustrate again what was demostrated in earliest human history—that divinely bestowed physical and mental advantage endure through many generations despite abuse or misuse.

One unanswered and unanswerable question, from our limited human viewpoint, is how long and how well some might live today if they made major efforts from earliest years to live in harmony with the laws of health.

"He [God] has established the laws of nature, but His laws are not arbitrary exactions. Every 'Thou shalt not,' whether in physical or moral law, contains or implies a promise. If it is obeyed, blessings will attend our steps; if it is disobeyed, the result is danger and unhappiness. The laws of God are designed to bring His people closer to Himself."[22]

"To many of the afflicted ones who received healing, Christ said, 'Sin no more, lest a worse thing come unto thee.' John 5:14. Thus He taught that disease is the result of violating God's laws, both natural and spiritual. The great misery in the world would not exist did men but live in harmony with the Creator's plan."[23]

"Courage, hope, faith, sympathy, love, promote health and prolong life. A contented mind, a cheerful spirit, is health to the body and strength to the soul. 'A merry [rejoicing] heart doeth good like a medicine.' Proverbs 17:22."[24]

If we allow God to write His law in our hearts, we will find it a delight to observe both His health laws and His moral law. The stronger the desire to live a completely sanctified life, the higher the level of healthful state we will attain, both physically and mentally. The Lord has promised, "The Lord will take away from thee all sickness, and will put none of the evil diseases . . . which thou knowest, upon thee."[25]

Jesus came to give us life and life more abundant. Eternal life also means a fullness of life in which man may enjoy—to the fullest extent—happiness, good health, a sense of achievement, the pleasures of friendship, excitement of discovery, and the unspeakable joy of communication with God face-to-face and progressing forever into a deeper understanding of His love.

1. Proverbs 17:22.
2. Ellen G. White, *Education*, pp. 196, 197.
3. Ellen G. White, *Christ's Object Lessons*, pp. 347, 348.
4. Ellen G. White, *Christ's Object Lessons*, p. 348.
5. Psalm 19:1, 7.
6. Ellen G. White, *Counsels to Teachers*, p. 186.
7. Exodus 19:16, 18.
8. Genesis 1:24.
9. Ellen G. White, *My Life Today*, p. 135.
10. Job 28:25, NIV.
11. *S.D.A Bible Commentary*, vol. 1, p. 757.
12. Ellen G. White, *The Desire of Ages*, p. 308.
13. Proverbs 23:7.
14. Matthew 5:17, 18.
15. Ellen G. White, *Patriarchs and Prophets*, p. 365.
16. 1 Corinthians 3:16, 17.
17. Exodus 15:26.
18. Ellen G. White, *Christ's Object Lessons*, p. 346.
19. Ellen G. White, *Counsels on Health*, p. 41.
20. Leviticus 11:44.
21. Ellen G. White, *The Ministry of Healing*, p. 241.
22. Ellen G. White, *Testimonies*, vol. 5, p. 445.
23. Ellen G. White, *The Desire of Ages*, p. 824.
24. Ellen G. White, *The Ministry of Healing*, p. 241.
25. Deuteronomy 7:15.

Maturity Through Inner Conflict

Before a sinner accepts the grace of Christ in faith, he lives a miserable life. At the moment he opens his heart to Jesus and accepts Him as a personal Saviour, his sins are forgiven. The burden of guilt on his heart is lifted; in God's sight he is a just man—sinless—because the righteousness of Christ has covered His sin.

From now on this disciple of Jesus can go on to live a sanctified life. However, the path of life is never a level, straight line. It goes up mountains, and it goes down into deep valleys. The path of spiritual life is likewise often a rough one. The experience of maturing in Christ is seldom smooth: a bitter war is fought on the battlefields of our hearts. The forces of good and of evil constantly engage in fierce conflict. In this kind of situation one learns the inner peace that results from belief in Christ's justifying righteousness, develops character, and learns the real power of the inward law.

Sandwiched between two great forces, we ourselves are powerless before both. It is impossible to win against Satan if help is not solicited from Christ. Worse yet, we are so prone to fall into Satan's snares and so inclined to sin that without intervening influences, our fate would seem to be sealed. However, we are not without hope. ''For what the law could not do, in that it was weak through the flesh, God sending his own Son in the likeness of sinful flesh, and for sin, condemned sin in the flesh: that the righteousness of the law might be fulfilled in us, who walk not after the flesh, but after the Spirit."[1] We are already victors by Christ's victory.

"The history of truth has ever been the record of a struggle between right and wrong. The proclamation of the gospel has ever been carried forward in this world in the face of opposition, peril, loss, and suffering."[2]

It is said that repeated similar choices form a habit, and a collection of habits forms a character. Even though one may have the intention of doing good, yet before he forms a good habit, he must—like a child learning to walk—deliberately concentrate all his attention and energy upon performing that task, lest he stumble. This is especially true when evil forces are at work to make whatever we do more difficult. But with the help of Christ—like a child learning to walk under the guidance of his mother—we steady our steps and we learn to walk. Similarly, we learn to talk, we learn to brush our teeth, we learn to play musical instruments, and we learn to perform many other duties efficiently. We form habits.

In the spiritual realm we also mature gradually by forming good habits. Once we form the habit of paying tithe, we need not struggle in our hearts over whether we should pay the whole tithe or just a part. In this aspect, Satan has no dominion over us. In like manner, by looking into the face of Christ, we learn to be kind, patient, considerate, temperate, optimistic, and to develop many other good traits.

Because of the evil forces constantly at work, the battle goes on all the time. Knowing that Christ's victory is counted as ours and accepting constantly the grace of God, we can form good habits and good characters. Our characters mature when we accept God's grace to help us with the struggles in our hearts—our lives become outworkings of the inward law.

While it is presumptuous for one to maintain that he himself has instantly attained perfection or has reached that state once and for all, perfection is still within our reach, for Jesus said, "Be ye therefore perfect, even as your Father which is in heaven is perfect."[3] This is both a command and a promise—a promise with heaven's full provision to back us in achieving this state.

Confucius once said, "I developed a desire to learn at fifteen. At thirty I stood (as a man); at forty my doubts were alleviated; at fifty I knew the decrees of heaven; at sixty my ear became an obedient organ (for the reception of truth—and yet deaf to rumors and slanders); at seventy I can follow what my good conscience desires, without transgressing that which is right."[4]

This confession of Confucius, who has been considered a great philosopher by the Chinese for twenty-five centuries, shows that he understood that the path to maturity is progressive.

All living creatures mature in stages. This is more obvious in the higher classes of plants and animals. Man, the crown of God's creation, takes about twenty years to mature fully—much longer than any other kind of animal. And man is even more pronounced than other animals in the characteristics or dimensions of each stage of his maturation. The development of motor skills, height increase, weight increase, the growth of hair, development of acne, and the wrinkling of the skin all signify the arrival of certain stages of physical development. So with spiritual growth.

The apostle Paul lists six different illustrations of spiritual growth—from death to life, from following the flesh to following the Spirit, from having a carnal mind to having a spiritual mind, from being at enmity with God to having peace with God, from a sinful state to a righteous state, and from being a slave to being a child of God with the freedom of enjoying all the good gifts He waits to bestow upon us.

The free gift of life in Christ is the only remedy that saves man from death. "The law of the Spirit of life in Christ Jesus hath made me free from the law of sin and death."[5] "For what the Law was unable to do, weakened as it was through the flesh, that God did by sending His own Son in the likeness of sinful flesh and on account of sin; He thus condemned sin in human nature."[6] When Jesus won the battle over sin on the

cross and over death in the
of the saints was sealed.

The Spirit is a life-giving
because He exercises life-gi
the Spirit of life is the life-
Spirit, ruling as a law in the
expresses the effect accompli
life' . . . [Romans 5:18] and
6:35). The Spirit brings life
with the law of sin, which
condemnation. . . .

"The law of sin and death. That is, the authority exercised by sin and ending in death. Sin is no longer the predominating and controlling influence in his life. The indwelling Spirit of life inspires obedience and gives power to 'mortify the deeds of the body' (v. 13.). Thus the law of the Spirit of life works directly contrary to the law of sin and death in the members, empowering the believer to overcome sin's destroying influence and freeing him from sin's bondage and condemnation."[7]

The law does not heal. "The law reveals to man his sins, but it provides no remedy. While it promises life to the obedient, it declares that death is the portion of the transgressor. The gospel of Christ alone can free him from the condemnation or the defilement of sin. He must exercise repentance toward God, whose law has been transgressed; and faith in Christ, his atoning sacrifice. Thus he obtains 'remission of sins that are past' and becomes a partaker of the divine nature. He is a child of God, having received the spirit of adoption, whereby he cries: 'Abba, Father!' "[8]

There is only one source of life—God. The apostle John tells us that "he that hath the son hath life: and he that hath not the Son of God hath not life."[9] "In him was life; and the life was the light of men."[10]

"In the new birth the heart is brought into harmony with God, as it is brought into accord with His law. When this mighty change has taken place in the sinner, he has passed from death unto life, from sin unto holiness."[11]

low God's inward law to be written in
e must follow the Holy Spirit's guidance.
s Son became man and lived a sinless life has
possible "that the righteousness of the law
be fulfilled in us, who walk not after the flesh, but
er the Spirit."[12]

"**After the Spirit.** That is, they regulate their conduct according to the dictates and guidance of the Spirit, the indwelling Spirit of Christ. . . . The just requirement of the law is being fulfilled in them. What the law requires is summed up in Christian love, for 'love is the fulfilling of the law.' . . . Likewise, the result of the working of the Holy Spirit in the life is love, for 'the fruit of the Spirit is love' (Gal. 5:22). Consequently, life according to the Spirit means a life in which the righteous demands of the law are fulfilled—a life of love and loving obedience. That such a life might be made possible for believers was the great purpose for which God sent His Son into the world."[13]

There must be an intent and a decision to expel from the soul the natural "inhabitants" that generate all evil works—the works of the flesh. Only then can there be an inflowing of the Holy Spirit to fill the vacancy. Both the expelling and the infilling are by the Spirit's power, but never overriding the will of the soul itself. Because of this there is no spiritual pride in the Spirit-filled heart. Rather, there is a growing sense of dependence upon the Spirit for the outworking of the inward law.

"The Spirit that reveals, also works in him the fruits of righteousness. Christ is in him, 'a well of water springing up into everlasting life.' He is a branch of the True Vine, and bears rich clusters of fruit to the glory of God. What is the character of the fruit borne?—The fruit of the Spirit is 'love,' not hatred, 'joy,' not discontent and mourning; 'peace,' not irritation, anxiety, and manufactured trials."[14]

In Romans 12 Paul tells us that we are to dedicate our body and mind together to God as a holy, living sacrifice, and the method of achieving this is by being transformed by the Spirit that we may discern God's perfect will for us. In other words, we are not to follow our own flesh, our own desires, our own natural tendencies, but to give them up and follow God, having a willingness to be directed by the Holy Spirit so that we can live a holy life.

"With what care should Christians regulate their habits, that they may preserve the full vigor of every faculty to give to the service of Christ. If we would be sanctified in soul, body, and spirit, we must live in conformity to the divine law. The heart cannot preserve consecration to God while the appetites and passions are indulged at the expense of health and life."[15]

Spiritual Mind Versus Carnal Mind

"To be carnally minded is death; but to be spiritually minded is life and peace."[16] **"To be carnally minded.** Literally, 'the mind [or "minding"] of the flesh.' In this case, 'mind' means 'thought,' 'purpose,' 'intention,' 'inclination,' as in the clause, 'he . . . knoweth what is the mind of the Spirit.' "[17]

Spiritual losses do not take place suddenly. As a general rule there is a series of small violations of the conscience that has a confusing impact on the mind and judgment. The distinction between good and evil becomes blurred. The voice of God is heard less and less distinctly, and the deceptions of Satan come to be accepted as enlightened wisdom. The soul is then in grave peril. And without a deliberate decision as to who is to be master of the soul, there will be inevitable and eternal loss.

"The carnal mind is enmity against God, and it rebels against His will. Let it once throw off the yoke of obedience and it slips unconsciously into the lawlessness of crime."[18]

"It is the Spirit that causes to shine into darkened minds the bright beams of the Sun of Righteousness; that makes men's hearts burn within them with an awakened realization of the truths of eternity; that presents before the mind the great standard of righteousness, and convinces of sin; that inspires faith in Him who alone can save from sin; that works to transform character by withdrawing the affections of men from those things which are temporal and perishable, and fixing them upon the eternal inheritance. The Spirit re-creates, refines, and sanctifies human beings, fitting them to become members of the royal family, children of the heavenly King."[19]

Only he who has lived in a home where two are basically not agreed can have any real idea of the level of cruelty that one who once professed loving devotion can impose on the former object of his affection. This is especially true if the "drifter" from God still has a troubled and accusing conscience. Similar cruelty will rain down upon God's true children in the final days of earth's history. Only the heart kept by the Spirit will retain loyalty to God in that climax of the ages.

"And you hath he quickened, who were dead in trespasses and sins; wherein in the time past ye walked according to the course of this world, according to the prince of the power of the air, the spirit that now worketh in the children of disobedience: among whom also we all had our conversation in times past in the lusts of the flesh and of the mind; and were by nature the children of wrath, even as others." "That at the time ye were without Christ, being aliens from the commonwealth of Israel, and strangers from the covenants of promise, having no hope, and without God in the world: but now in Christ Jesus ye who sometimes were far off are made nigh by the blood of Christ. For he is our peace, who hath made both one, and hath broken down the middle wall of partition between us; having abolished in his flesh the enmity, even the law of commandments contained in ordinances; for to make in himself of twain one new man, so making peace; and that he might reconcile both unto God in one body by the cross, having slain the enmity thereby."[20]

Peace versus Enmity

"To be spiritually minded is life and peace. Because

the carnal mind is enmity against God: for it is not subject to the law of God, neither indeed can be.''[21] It is tragic ever to have to think of man as the enemy of God, when he was made in God's image with every advantage and faculty for retaining a position of loving loyalty to the inward law implanted in his nature. But such is the sad consequence of the first transgression of the law of God. Ever since then the carnal mind has been at enmity with God, for it is not submissive to His law and cannot be.[22]

But if man will look in the mirror of the law of God as revealed in the life of Jesus here on earth, he will see himself as a sinner under the penalty of the sacred law. But he need not despair. He has not been abandoned— not left an orphan. The Son of God on Calvary has provided a way of deliverance from sin's penalty and its power. For this purpose God gave His only-begotten Son.[23]

''Shortly before His crucifixion Christ had bequeathed to His disciples a legacy of peace. 'Peace I leave with you,' He said, 'My peace I give unto you: not as the world giveth, give I unto you. Let not your heart be troubled, neither let it be afraid.' John 14:27. This peace is not the peace that comes through conformity to the world. Christ never purchased peace by compromise. The peace that Christ left His disciples is internal rather than external and was ever to remain with His witnesses through strife and contention.

''Christ said of Himself, 'Think not that I am come to send peace on earth: I came not to send peace, but a sword.' Matthew 10:34. The Prince of Peace, He was yet the cause of division. He who came to proclaim glad tidings and to create hope and joy in the hearts of the children of men, opened a controversy that burns deep and arouses intense passion in the human heart.''[24]

In order to make a peace treaty effective, both sides must observe its details. In order to maintain our peaceful relationship with God, we must observe our covenant with Him, the Ten Commandments, which, if we permit them to be written on our hearts as our inward law, will become our peace treaty with God. "Therefore if any man be in Christ, he is a new creature: old things are passed away; behold, all things are become new. And all things are of God, who hath reconciled us to himself by Jesus Christ, and hath given to us the ministry of reconciliation; to wit, that God was in Christ, reconciling the world unto himself, not imputing their trespasses unto them; and hath committed unto us the word of reconciliation."[25] This reconciliation Jesus performed "in the body of his flesh through death, to present you holy and unblameable and unreproveable in his sight."[26]

Righteousness versus Sin

"If Christ be in you, the body is dead because of sin; but the Spirit is life because of righteousness."[27]

"Throughout the Scriptures righteousness is consistently associated with life, as sin is with death. When there is righteousness in the life, there is evidence of the presence and power of the Spirit of God, and this means life.

"Some commentators prefer to limit the meaning of righteousness in this passage to the righteousness of Christ imputed to the believer for life-giving justification. . . . But the context does not seem to indicate such a limitation. Taking righteousness in the widest sense, Paul's meaning seems to be that, although the body is dead because of Adam's sin, in which we have all participated . . . , the spirit is life because of Christ's righteousness, which has first been imputed in justification and is later imparted in sanctification. This gift of righteousness is accompanied by the gift of eternal life."[28]

Holiness is simply wholeness for God—a total surrender to the working out of the inward law by God's grace. So holiness is not inherited; neither is it the gift of the most capable human. Holiness is the gift of God through Jesus Christ alone. When we receive Him, we become members of God's family—born again, renewed in righteousness. Our very minds are changed so that we can perceive eternal realities. As adopted children, we come to resemble our Father more and more under the Spirit's transforming power.

But since we are still sinners our own righteousness cannot be presented to God because it is as filthy rags. Nevertheless, we can develop, by the grace of God, a greater yearning for spiritual things. Through Bible study and prayer we can accept more of Christ's righteousness until we are being filled up with Christ.

Both in our conversion and in the life experience of transforming grace and power, it is the absolute righteousness of Jesus Christ that purchases, through the cross, our complete acceptance with God.

"The work of transformation from unholiness to holiness is a continuous one. Day by day God labors for man's sanctification, and man is to cooperate with Him, putting forth persevering efforts in the cultivation of right habits. He is to add grace to grace; and as he thus works on the plan of addition, God works for him on the plan of multiplication."[29]

The Bible uses a white robe to symbolize the righteousness of Christ. We are told to put on the robe of the righteousness of Christ. But this metaphor can only partially reveal to us the wonderful working of God's plan. Yes, we must *put on* the righteousness of Christ, yet we can also *enter into* the righteousness of Christ; and we can even allow the righteousness of Christ to fill our hearts and to *permeate* every part of our body. While these illustrations are all good ones and each describes the working of the Holy Spirit, we must not be limited by the particular meaning of a certain word. We must allow the Holy Spirit to guide our minds, that our understanding of spiritual things may be progressively deepened. The limited meaning of any word must not hinder our understanding of God's wonderful plan of salvation.

Children versus Slaves

"Ye have not received the spirit of bondage again to fear; but ye have received the Spirit of adoption, whereby we cry, Abba, Father.''[30]

''The dearest gift that heaven itself had to bestow has been poured out that God 'might be just, and the justifier of him which believeth in Jesus.' By that gift men are uplifted from the ruin and degradation of sin to become children of God. Says Paul: 'Ye have received the Spirit of adoption, whereby we cry, Abba, Father.'

''Brethren, with the beloved John I call upon you to 'behold, what manner of love the Father hath bestowed upon us, that we should be called the sons of God.' What love, what matchless love, that, sinners and aliens as we are, we may be brought back to God and adopted into His family! We may address Him by the endearing name, 'Our Father,' which is a sign of our affection for Him and a pledge of His tender regard and relationship to us.''[31]

If we really understand the meaning of Matthew 6:9 and address God as Jesus taught us to do, we will be freed from slavery to become free children of God. Our relationship with God will change completely, and our relationship to our neighbors will become that of brothers and sisters. Through love, we break the shackles of Satan. The bondage we were under is now broken by God's love, by His spiritual adoption, whereby we have become His children.

''Every soul that refuses to give himself to God is under the control of another power. He is not his own. He may talk of freedom, but he is in the most abject slavery. He is not allowed to see the beauty of truth, for his mind is under the control of Satan. While he flatters himself that he is following the dictates of his own judgment, he obeys the will of the prince of darkness. Christ came to break the shackles of sin-slavery from the soul. 'If the Son therefore shall make you free, ye shall be free indeed.' [John 8:36.]''[32]

The righteousness of Jesus Christ and His sacrificial death on our behalf vindicates our adoption into the family of God. This remains the only basis of salvation—acceptance in and through the divine Substitute. Having been adopted, we prostrate ourselves in joy and gratitude at His feet, crying, "Lord, what wilt Thou have me do?" He shows us and empowers the restoraton of the inward law in our whole being.

When we are truly and constantly aware of our sonship or daughtership in Christ, we will long to be like Him. We will love to do His will; His law will have become our inward law. We will discard our own likes and dislikes, our selfish idiosyncracies, our evil habits, and our all, in order to accept all from Him. In doing so, sin will have no dominion over us and we will be free indeed. In life eternal all saints will enjoy a perfect love relationship with God, with men, with angels, and with creatures of other worlds. Should we not start now to allow God to write on our hearts His law, that we may gradually mature into such a state that God can accept us into His kingdom forever and ever?

1. Romans 8:3, 4.
2. Ellen G. White, *The Acts of the Apostles*, p. 85.
3. Matthew 5:48.
4. *Confucian Analect*.
5. Romans 8:2.
6. Romans 8:3, Modern Language Bible (Berkeley).
7. *S.D.A. Bible Commentary*, vol. 6, p. 560.
8. Ellen G. White, *The Great Controversy*, pp. 467, 468.
9. 1 John 5:12.
10. John 1:4.
11. Ellen G. White, *The Great Controversy*, p. 468.
12. Romans 8:4.
13. *S.D.A. Bible Commentary*, vol. 6, p. 562.
14. Ellen G. White, *Gospel Workers*, p. 287.
15. Ellen G. White, *Counsels on Health*, p. 69.
16. Romans 8:6.
17. *S.D.A. Bible Commentary*, vol. 6, p. 563.
18. Ellen G. White, *Testimonies*, vol. 4, p. 13.
19. Ellen G. White, *Gospel Workers*, pp. 286, 287.
20. Ephesians 2:1-3, 12-16.
21. Romans 8:6, 7.
22. See Romans 8:7.
23. See John 3:16.
24. Ellen G. White, *The Acts of the Apostles*, p. 84.
25. 2 Corinthians 5:17-19.
26. Colosians 1:22.
27. Romans 8:10.
28. *S.D.A. Bible Commentary*, vol. 6, p. 565.
29. Ellen G. White, *The Acts of the Apostles*, p. 532.
30. Romans 8:15.
31. Ellen G. White, *Testimonies*, vol. 5, pp. 739, 740.
32. Ellen G. White, *The Desire of Ages*, p. 466.